Contents

PART FOUR
CRITICAL HISTORY

PART FIVE
BACKGROUND

PART ONE

INTRODUCTION

HOW TO STUDY A POEM

Studying on your own requires self-discipline and a carefully thought-out work plan in order to be effective.

- Poetry is the most challenging kind of literary writing. In your first reading you may well not understand what the poem is about. Don't jump too swiftly to any conclusions about the poem's meaning.
- Read the poem many times, and including out loud. After the second or third reading, write down any features you find interesting or unusual.
- What is the poem's **tone** of voice? What is the poem's mood?
- Does the poem have an argument? Is it descriptive?
- Is the poet writing in his or her own voice? Might he or she be using a **persona** or mask?
- Is there anything special about the kind of language the poet has chosen? Which words stand out? Why?
- What elements are repeated? Consider **alliteration, assonance, rhyme,** rhythm, **metaphor** and ideas.
- What might the poem's **images** suggest or symbolise?
- What might be significant about the way the poem is arranged in lines? Is there a regular pattern of lines? Does the grammar coincide with the ending of the lines or does it 'run over'? What is the effect of this?
- Do not consider the poem in isolation. Can you compare and contrast the poem with any other work by the same poet or with any other poem that deals with the same theme?
- What do you think the poem is about?
- Every argument you make about the poem must be backed up with details and quotations that explore its language and organisation.
- Always express your ideas in your own words.

These York Notes offer an introduction to the poetry of Carol Ann Duffy and cannot substitute for close reading of the text and the study of secondary sources.

CONTEXT

The word 'poetry' comes from the Greek word *poesis*, meaning 'making' or 'creating'. People have been writing poetry for thousands of years – the earliest we have dates back to c.3000BC.

READING CAROL ANN DUFFY'S POETRY

CONTEXT

Twentieth-century poetry in the mid to late 1980s was characterised, among other things, by the large number of new voices emerging, many of whom were women.

One of the most significant features of Carol Ann Duffy's poetry, and one for which she is justly famed, is the use of the **dramatic monologue**. Intimately linked to this is her exceptionally acute ear for the voice of the people she presents. Another aspect of her poetry is the strikingly fresh use of **imagery**. Some of the themes she explores are relationships, sexuality, politics, religion, memory, loss, the effects of time, and the marginalising of women. There is a great deal to be gained from following the trends in the development of her writing. *Standing Female Nude*, her first collection, clearly sets an agenda, one rooted in what is clearly a feminist position but a feminism that should not be simplistically interpreted as an anti-male position (see **Background: Feminism**).

The range of Carol Ann Duffy's poetry is wide. She is able to engage with important philosophical concerns, write with acute wit and humour, and respond sympathetically to the isolated and oppressed members of society. Hers is a poetry rooted in common experience, but its accessibility belies its complexity and richly **allusive** nature. While clearly speaking in a highly distinctive modern voice, Carol Ann Duffy is acutely aware of the heritage of English, American and European poetry. Her debt to Robert Browning (1812–89) is clear in her extensive use of the dramatic monologue. John Keats (1795–1821) was an early interest and she consciously tried to imitate him as a very young person. His influence is not immediately obvious, but her sensualism indicates an affinity with him. Carol Ann Duffy read and admired Gerard Manley Hopkins (1844–89) for his acute observation and technical mastery. The French poets Arthur Rimbaud (1854–91) and Charles Baudelaire (1821–67) also formed part of her reading. The Englishness of W. H. Auden (1907–73) is very much at the heart of his appeal for Carol Ann Duffy, as is his versatile use of traditional poetic forms. Female poets such as Sylvia Plath (1932–63) and Adrienne Rich (1929–) were read avidly. Sylvia Plath's extraordinary control of language and use of imagery made a lasting impact while Adrienne Rich's radicalism offered a challenging example to Carol Ann Duffy's own emergent feminist position.

Perhaps the most powerful poetic influence on her work is that of T. S. Eliot. For a more detailed consideration of Carol Ann Duffy's work in its historical and cultural context, see **Background**.

A number of her poems deal with the limitations, as well as the possibilities, of language. It is hardly surprising that language should be a major preoccupation of a person whose life is devoted to exploring its potentials, but it is notable that Duffy frequently draws attention to its inability to convey what human beings wish to express. There is a constant preoccupation with truth too. Because of the richness of her writing, the poems offer an entertaining, challenging and worthwhile experience for the reader. They repay close study and reveal an incisive mind and formidable poetic talent at work.

CHECK THE BOOK

For a detailed commentary about the influence of T. S. Eliot on Duffy's poetry, see Neil Roberts's essay 'Duffy, Eliot and impersonality' in *The Poetry of Carol Ann Duffy: 'Choosing Tough Words'*, edited by Angelica Michelis and Antony Rowland, pp. 33–46 (2003).

PART TWO

THE TEXT

NOTE ON THE TEXT

Carol Ann Duffy has published six collections of poems for adults: *Standing Female Nude* (1985), *Selling Manhattan* (1987), *The Other Country* (1990), *Mean Time* (1993), *The World's Wife* (1999) and *Feminine Gospels* (2002). Her *New Selected Poems 1984–2004* was published by Picador in 2004, marking the twentieth year of her remarkable writing career. She has also published three pamphlets: *Thrown Voices* (1986), *William and the Ex-Prime Minister* (1992) and *The Pamphlet* (1998).

Duffy has emerged as one of the most gifted **lyric** poets of our time. She is well known for her skilful use of the **dramatic monologue,** as well as her versatility in the handling of traditional poetic forms and **free verse.**

There are clear developments in the concerns expressed in each collection. The poems discussed in these Notes have been selected with a view to demonstrating the breadth and depth of her work. Where necessary or appropriate, reference is made to poems not included in *New Selected Poems 1984–2004.* Although *Standing Female Nude* was published in 1985, the collection was completed in 1984, which explains the time span of *New Selected Poems.*

DETAILED SUMMARIES

STANDING FEMALE NUDE

As a debut collection, *Standing Female Nude* had a major impact when it was published in 1985. The poems in it reveal an acutely observant poet whose concerns are those shared by almost everyone. They range from explorations of love and loss to politics, religion, education, art, childhood and memory. One of the most

CONTEXT

The Conservative Party had won a second term in office in 1983. *Standing Female Nude* gives voice to political frustrations that become more explicit in later collections.

arresting features of her writing is the consummate ease with which she is able to marshal numerous voices in her dramatic monologues, a writing technique for which she has become widely celebrated. There is a clear commitment to giving voice to female perspectives on life, but at no point could Carol Ann Duffy be described as antipathetic to men in a general sense. She is sensitive to the disaffected but is quick to expose the unacceptably aggressive sexism of men.

Unadorned, female independence is clearly stressed in the title of the collection. The woman who stands up is confident and assertive, while her nudity indicates that she feels no need to cover herself in any way. In particular, she will not conform to the expectations of men. In this way she is making the objects of male-orientated aspects of society autonomous subjects of her own art which, in its turn, interrogates those very aspects. Alongside the general gender debate there are particular areas of concern relating to the Church. Rejecting the Catholicism into which she was born, Duffy presents this as restrictive, intolerant, unsympathetic and male-dominated.

Many of the themes addressed in *Standing Female Nude* are developed in later collections. The issue of sexuality is quite prominent among these and is mentioned here in the context of sexual politics as well as interpersonal relationships. In 'Ash Wednesday 1984' Duffy alludes to homosexuality and she explores this more extensively in, for example, 'Warming Her Pearls' (*Selling Manhattan*); 'Two Small Poems of Desire' (*The Other Country*); 'Café Royal' (*Mean Time*).

Another feature of Duffy's writing is her confident employment of traditional forms. In particular, she is adept at employing the **sonnet** for both narrative and descriptive purposes.

CHECK THE BOOK

Carol Ann Duffy by Deryn Rees-Jones (1999) contains a fine commentary on 'Standing Female Nude' and Duffy's work up to *The Pamphlet* (1998).

STANDING FEMALE NUDE

- A woman models for a painter who hopes to become famous; she has a very cynical view of what he is.
- A prostitute, she poses for him in order to supplement her income.
- Her assessment of him does not correspond to that made by people who claim to be able to appreciate art.

 CHECK THE NET
Use a comprehensive online encyclopedia such as **http://en. wikipedia.org** to find out more about cubism.

Providing the title for her first collection, 'Standing Female Nude' is only one of a number of Carol Ann Duffy's poems inspired by paintings. In this case the work in question is *Nude* (1907) by the cubist painter Georges Braque (1882–1963).

COMMENTARY

The poem is a **dramatic monologue** in the voice of a French woman who is forced by poverty into prostitution. The economic forces acting upon her and the artist are similar: 'Both poor, we make our living how we can' (stanza 4). There is some **ambivalence** in her attitude to him. On the whole she is contemptuous of his exploitative treatment of her but she understands that they both face harsh economic realities. He stands to become wealthy if the picture of a poor woman becomes popular with the rich who 'coo' at the sight of the painting. The subjects of art become objects of exploitation and a tension is set up. Both processes result, potentially, in the woman being 'possessed' by men in some way.

Despite the fact that the woman may seem to be in the thrall of men, there is a clear sense that she has a good deal of power. The artist is presented as a rather inadequate figure: 'Little man, / you've not the money for the arts I sell' (stanza 4). The word 'Little' not only suggests a reduction in status but is also sexually dismissive. There is an implied comparison here with bigger men, but even they are in one sense cut down to size because prostitution itself can be thought of as an index of the way men cannot contain their sexual urges. Neither can some of them achieve sexual release except by paying for it. The defiant close of the poem, 'It does not look like me', reminds us that the artist is not concerned to be faithfully representational.

More forcefully, we hear his work being assessed by the one person who should be qualified to do so with any authority. 'They call it Art' is provisionally dismissive of what is potentially mere exploitation and voyeuristic interest in 'an image of a river whore' (stanza 1). There is ambivalence communicated in the one-word sentence at the start of stanza 2: 'Maybe.' It suggests that the woman does have a degree of aesthetic response even though she may be sceptical about it. Whatever her true feelings, she is able to observe the painter's technique and report aspects of it: 'He is concerned with volume, space, / I with the next meal' (stanza 2).

The presentation of 'the Queen of England' in the gallery, 'Magnificent, she murmurs, / moving on' (stanza 2), suggests that she is merely saying what she feels is expected, oblivious to the economic subjection of the model. The real woman speaks in place of the mute canvas of herself that will be displayed like meat 'hung / in great museums'.

CONTEXT

The earlier phase of cubism was sometimes called 'analytic'.

The woman says, 'I shall be represented analytically' (line 5), drawing attention to a means of looking at a woman from a male artist's point of view. Here, Duffy actually turns the terminology to feminist advantage by making her sarcasm heard in the model's voice. This is wholly consistent with the presentation of contempt for the man who is thought by the 'bourgeoisie' to be a 'genius'. Through the casual tone of the woman we begin to hear her defiance, not to mention awareness.

Crucially, the poem is about the way a male appears to be 'possessing' a woman on canvas. It is not simply a process of representation that the poet explores. She also shows how the artist appropriates the woman for his purposes. In turn, the bourgeoisie will appropriate the image as part of their culture, thus making the original subject an object of transaction.

Carol Ann Duffy subverts the male artist who makes capital out of representing the female form. 'Standing Female Nude' becomes a

CONTEXT

Georges Braque (1882–1963) was a French cubist painter. The cubists formed the first group of abstract artists. They were given their name by Louis Vauxelles, a French art critic who remembered Matisse's remark about Braque's 'little cubes'. This referred to his geometrical technique of representing objects, people and landscapes as multifaceted solids. The early cubist works of both Braque and Pablo Picasso (1881–1973) have been called proto-cubist by some art critics. The mid-phase of the cubists known as 'hermetic' was characterised by monochromatic paintings in grey, blue, brown or white. This explains the literal sense in which the painter 'drains the colour' from his subject.

powerful slogan or manifesto statement spoken in the voice of the woman. It signifies a confident, uninhibited stance in a world where women are all too often marginalised or required, **metaphorically**, to remain seated. Also, the poem itself is an artistic construct, which interrogates power structures in society. Sexual politics and economic imperatives inform these relationships in ways that are both explicit and implicit. Although the woman is presented 'analytically' and it is she who uses the vocabulary of titillation, 'Belly nipple arse', she remains nameless and it is the man who, significantly, is named and stands to become famous for representing her. Art is capable of transcending class and gender boundaries, but as product or artefact becomes a commodity. By extension, its subjects are part of an economic transaction. Such works cannot be anything but anonymous without rich people to promote them.

The contrast in perspective between the man and woman is emphasised in the language they use. She is much more direct and refers to parts of her own body in graphic terms: 'Belly nipple arse … breasts'. All of these are anatomical details but are sexualised. The artist, though, is 'concerned with volume, space'. In spite of himself he is aroused by the woman and 'stiffens'. A direct sexual relationship is not possible between them because he cannot afford her rates. This emphasises sex as commodity rather than as expression of spontaneous passion. His desire for her is shown symbolically through the way he 'dips the brush / repeatedly into the paint' (stanza 3). The sexual **connotations** here are clear. Also, there is a post-coital implication in 'When it's finished, / … lights a cigarette.' The financial, transactional basis of their relationship is again emphasised by the woman's statement, 'I say / Twelve francs', as, significantly, she covers her nudity before dismissing the painting with the words 'It does not look like me.' This statement could well indicate the inability of the woman to understand what Georges the 'genius' is producing, but it might also be an **ironic** warning against pseudo-intellectualism.

WAR PHOTOGRAPHER

- A war photographer is described developing images in his darkroom.
- The editor of the newspaper he works for will select photos from these for inclusion in a Sunday supplement.
- Carol Ann Duffy is fascinated by what makes someone do such a job and how they feel about being in situations where a choice often has to be made between recording horrific events and helping.

Photographic images of war are common but those of certain photographers like McCullin (1935–) have become very famous. Although there is no definite attempt to recreate a scene from any specific photograph, one well-known image is suggested by the description in stanza 2 of the little girl running down a road, naked and terrified, having been burnt by napalm following an American attack on the village of Trang Bang in 1972. The photograph, taken by Nick Ut, is one of the most arresting and shocking images ever published by a photojournalist.

COMMENTARY

The poet does not immediately present us with the horror of war but chooses to take us into the photographer's darkroom. He is rather like a priest in that the development of the images in his darkroom has an air of ritual about it. The paraphernalia he uses are a secular analogue to those used by a priest involved in the conduct of Mass. The 'spools' are set out in 'ordered rows' just as the priest sets out chalice, ciborium and paten.

The red light is suggestive of a sanctuary light that always burns in a Catholic church to signify the Real Presence of Christ. In photographic spheres it is known as a safe light. This prevents black and white prints from fogging, but there is also a sense that the darkroom is a haven from the actual horror while also being the means by which the graphic memory of it may be seen by the

> **CONTEXT**
>
> The idea for the poem arose out of conversations with the famous war photographer, Don McCullin.

> **CONTEXT**
>
> In the 1970s, photographers like Don McCullin, Nick Ut and Eddie Adams were responsible for bringing the real horror of the Vietnam War to the world's attention. President Richard Nixon's time in office was blighted by America's protracted involvement.

photographer. He takes sanctuary in his darkroom just as someone might in a church.

Instead of 'preparing to intone a Mass' the photographer develops images of war. The final line of the first stanza reads like a litany of horror. Carol Ann Duffy's use of frequent full stops helps to fix (the final phase of the black and white printing process) each place in the mind of the reader. The litany of death in purely secular terms modulates seamlessly into the biblical quotation: 'All flesh is as grass'. Three well-known sites of war are concentrated into one line: Northern Ireland, the Middle East and Vietnam. The **alliteration** of 'Belfast' and 'Beirut', through sound identity, links places separated by great distances but suffering atrocity in the same way. The poet is reflecting upon mortality in a way that suggests people as sacrificial victims of war. This is aligned to the idea of the Mass being a commemoration of the sacrifice of Christ's life.

The **ambiguity** of the **onomatopoeic** 'Solutions slop in trays' in stanza 2 captures the sounds made by chemicals in which the photographs develop during the process and also signals that their production could help to arrest some suffering by the fact of their publication. Equally, though, it could be that there is irony in that there is no solution to the futility of war. In the safety of 'Rural England' it is difficult to imagine that the horrors of Vietnam, where landmines blow people's legs off and children are burnt by napalm 'in a nightmare heat', are real. The very process in which the photographer is involved is concerned with keeping such awful events vividly alive. The opening sentence of stanza 3 – 'Something is happening' – injects drama and suspense into a situation so as to suggest that the photographer is not in total control. Anyone who has seen a photograph develop will identify with what seems to be an almost miraculous happening. This recalls the likening, in the first stanza, of the photographer to a priest.

The sensitivity of the photographer is emphasised in the way he is affected by the memories provoked by the development of his images: 'He remembers the cries / of this man's wife' (stanza 3). He recalls his moral predicament as he 'sought approval / without words' to take the photograph of what presumably was the killing

CONTEXT

'All flesh is grass' echoes the First Letter of Peter in the New Testament of the Bible, 1:24–5: 'All flesh is as grass ... but the word of the Lord will endure for ever'.

www. CHECK THE NET

For sites exploring the work of war photographers mentioned by Carol Ann Duffy, search **http:// digitaljournalist. org** or **http://news. bbc.co.uk** or **http://www. tvcameramen. com** of her husband. He clearly feels that he 'must' do his job and that the best help that can be offered is often to take the photograph in order to bring atrocity to public attention.

There is a contrast drawn between the relative impact made by the images on the man who produces them and on the people who see his work. From the viewpoint of a newspaper editor, who from 'A hundred agonies in black-and-white / ... will pick out five or six / for Sunday's supplement', there is not much beyond the transactional. The people who look at the photographs in the newspaper do not seem to care. Having been bombarded with image after horrifying image they become inured or desensitised to what is presented to them. They might be moved 'between the bath and pre-lunch beers' but are cocooned in their safety.

The poem is about an **image** maker and, unsurprisingly, Duffy concentrates very much on the visual dimension. This leads to a reflection on the morality of those who commission the work of photojournalists, people who are almost invariably passionate about wanting to tell the truth in pictures. The poet traces this thought process and develops a line of thinking in sympathy with the process of photographic development. Through concrete detail she addresses in words what photographers confront with their cameras. The final **couplet** presents the reader with a wide-angle shot of the photographer flying over 'where / he earns his living'. The fact that he 'stares impassively' suggests that he has no feeling for this place and so it can be concluded that this is England. He cares deeply about the war zones of the world and about the indifference of the photographer's intended audience. The final words of the poem, 'they do not care', leave the reader with an image of bitter truth.

> **? QUESTION**
>
> How does Duffy use language associated with religion and ritual in this poem?

SHOOTING STARS

- A dead Jewish woman speaks to another about the atrocity and suffering she and her race have endured.

CONTEXT

More than six
million Jews were
murdered in the
death camps
using a gas called
Zyklon B. It was
very common,
though, for
prisoners to be
shot on the whim
of a German
soldier.

CONTEXT

During the Second
World War, the
German Nazis
implemented
a systematic
programme of
murder on an
industrial scale in
their death camps
such as Auschwitz.

This poem is a contemplation upon the Jewish victims of the
Holocaust in the Second World War, and it warns us about the
dangers of forgetting such a crime. The star of David is a potent
national **symbol** for Jews. A yellow star of David was used by the
Nazis as an identification badge on Jewish prisoners' clothing.
This had the effect of appropriating a cherished emblem of cultural
identity for horrific purposes. Even more horrific was the tattooing
of people with the symbol as an easy means of identification. As
Shylock in *The Merchant of Venice* by William Shakespeare says,
'suffrance is the badge of all our tribe' (I.3.105). The story of the
Jewish people has been one of almost unremitting persecution.

COMMENTARY

The **ambiguity** of the title is important. The stars on the prisoners'
clothing and bodies are one obvious signification, while there is also a
sense of the temporary nature of life in the **metaphorical** comparison
of people to meteors that we call shooting stars. There is a third
interpretation – that outstanding individuals have been annihilated.

The first stanza presents the words of a victim of the Nazis who will
'no longer speak', a **euphemistic** way of saying that she is dead. The
poem, of course, reanimates her dead voice. The woman's wedding
ring is 'salvage[d]', indicating that her tormentors value her life less
than the gold ring. She, however, values the ring for its symbolic
and personal significance and not for the money it might fetch. Her
fingers are broken in order to achieve this salvaging, creating the
impression of a scrap heap being picked over. She says that there are
stars of David tattooed on the prisoners' foreheads; these provide a
shocking target for the soldiers who will literally be shooting stars.
She can protest for ever as the poem gives her voice eternal life. The
list of Jewish forenames, possibly her children, draws attention to
their cultural identity and reinforces the idea that there is no need
for further identifying marks to be applied to them by their
antagonists. Here, then, is a stark contrast between the simple
dignity of names proclaiming the individual, and the stripping
away of that dignity.

Stanzas 2 and 3 explore further the atrocities visited on the victims
of war and the heroic bravery of the women who suffered at the

hands of the Nazis. Their stoical endurance allowed them to wait for their deaths 'upright as statues' but there is also a clear implication that they could be frozen with terror. We are familiar with the word 'petrified' to describe extreme fear; it derives from the Greek word *petros*, meaning rock. Statues, being generally made of stone, fit the scene Duffy is exploring most effectively.

The woman addresses her friend, reminding her of how she faced death, how she 'Fell'. This word simultaneously conjures up the picture of her friend slumping to the ground after being shot and also reminds us of its frequent use as a euphemism in time of war. To fall in wartime is to die in battle. This is horrific enough in itself but we are presented here with women who were not even combatants; they were defenceless and powerless. The woman, whose voice sounds throughout the poem, is emphatic about the fact that she wants such atrocity to be remembered: 'I say, Remember. / Remember these appalling days which make the world / forever bad.' Duffy uses repetition for emphasis but, more subtly, capitalises 'Remember' at the end of a sentence as she is drawing attention to the vital status of cultural collective memory. Also, the crucial need for the whole world to avoid a repetition of the Holocaust is paramount. From the **persona**'s perspective, however, there is no redemptive possibility, as the world is perceived as 'forever bad'.

The third stanza deals with the crime of rape. The sheer terror of the woman is vividly conveyed through Carol Ann Duffy's concentration on its physical effects: 'My bowels opened in a ragged gape of fear.' The word 'gape' is often used to describe a facial expression, and this makes the effacement of the woman's identity by such brutality even more shocking. The hopeless surrender to fear is momentarily mediated, though, in the glimpsed child through the 'gap' the woman can see between 'corpses'. The child, embodiment of life and hope for the future, is wickedly murdered: 'They shot her in the eye.' These events are no more than amusement for the soldiers, who are intoxicated by power which expresses itself in sexual attacks and the indiscriminate execution of civilians. Of course, it is a recurring feature of war that occupying armies use rape of women and the murder of children as a means of

CHECK THE BOOK

Primo Levi's *If This Is a Man* is required reading (1947). In it Levi writes about his harrowing experiences in Auschwitz. Sadly, he committed suicide on 11 April 1987.

inflicting shame on another culture. Reports of atrocities in Kosovo in 1999 tell us that Serbian soldiers enjoyed killing and raping just as the Germans referred to in the poem 'laughed'. The time frame referred to in this stanza therefore has eerie connections with the political climate in parts of Europe at the close of the twentieth century, and in the Middle East at the opening of the twenty-first. The woman's observation that 'Only a matter of days separate / this from acts of torture now' suggests both eyewitness involvement at the time – 'this' and 'now' reinforce the sense of immediacy – and an awareness that memory is very short in historical terms. If only 'days separate' one atrocity from another, then the passage of years will make the repetition of such atrocities more possible. The woman's words assume a prophetic status when we consider the countless examples of war crimes since the close of the Second World War in 1945.

Stanza 4 explicitly poses a question already implicit in the previous three: 'How would you prepare to die …?' The counterpointed impulses of life and death are presented in the season of spring in nature, 'a perfect April evening' and the ominous 'graves'. The fear of rape is replaced by the fear of being shot. The sadistic soldier toys with his victim: 'I heard the click. Not yet. A trick.' This sees Carol Ann Duffy using short sentences at the end of the line to create both tension and a sense of the real experience of the woman and the power wielded by the soldier. The **internal rhyme** – 'trickled', 'click' and 'trick' – rolls easily off the tongue, and recreates the unexpected near silence surrounding the moment. This heightens the impression of mental torture and emphasises the complete contrast with the soldier who can view such an appalling act as a game. The woman's 'bare feet felt the earth', indicating that she was sensitive to it, in direct contrast to the jackbooted, unfeeling and desensitised aggressors.

Stanza 5 invites us to question how any real normality can return after such horror but also to remember that it does, and frighteningly quickly. The use of **anaphora** is striking, the repetition of 'After' emphasising that terrible things have actually happened but are almost immediately effaced. People can soon return to such familiar domesticity associated with 'tea on the lawn'

CHECK THE BOOK

Thomas Keneally's novel *Schindler's Ark* (1982) and Steven Spielberg's film based on it, *Schindler's List* (1993), starring Liam Neeson, Ben Kingsley and Ralph Fiennes, are moving insights into this terrible period in history.

just as a 'boy' can wash a uniform. This could be an ambiguous use of the words as many soldiers were little more than boys and a uniform can be worn by schoolboys, too. Whatever the case, there is a clear sense that the memory of 'terrible moans', representative of all the suffering in war, can be washed away, cleansed as simply as the Nazis thought they could erase the Jews. Children may be taught about the war in school but they 'run to their toys'. As children, they might be forgiven for this but there is no excuse for a world that 'turns in its sleep', wilfully ignoring the truth of a past that we ignore at our peril. The **alliteration** of sibilants phonically represents sleeping forgetfulness, while the reintroduction of Jewish forenames reminds us that the Holocaust was real. The **ellipsis** at the end of the stanza is a further stark reminder that the list of names could go on and on and almost amounts to another world. There is a depressing presentation of a world that finds it easy to forget.

The final stanza takes us back to the interior of a concentration camp. The woman addresses her 'Sister', a term more of cultural and religious significance that the simply familial. Her reference to singing 'inside the wire' indicates her bravery and defiance. She champions the culture she was born into and will not be subject to 'ethnic cleansing', a term that has unfortunately become widely used and, worse, validated by the media. The 'ancient psalms' referred to are from the Old Testament in the Bible. They have particular significance for the Jewish people. In the first place a psalm is a song, and communal singing is an important aspect of cultural assertion. Second, many of the psalms share themes of forbearance and strength in the face of adversity, as well as absolute faith in God as deliverer. The idea of a promised land is well known, and Moses is reputed to have led his people to such a place. Carol Ann Duffy chooses to end the poem with a quotation suggestive of anything but hope and deliverance. The twenty-fifth psalm, one of King David's, pleads with God for deliverance from affliction, shame and death: 'let not my enemies exult over me' (verse 2); 'Oh guard my life, and deliver me; / let me not be put to shame, for I / take refuge in thee' (verse 20). The woman keeps faith with her religion and tradition but her words at the end of the poem articulate the most desperate facet of the psalm she quotes from. In many ways we

CHECK THE NET

Search a comprehensive online encyclopedia such as **http://en.wikipedia.org** for useful information and links on Primo Levi.

might view the world today as 'desolate and lost' because it is so riven with war and factionalism. Persecution of minorities seems no less prevalent now than in the days during which the 'ancient psalms' were written, cataloguing as they do the travails and hopes of a nation. The final lines of Psalm 25: 'Redeem Israel, O God, / out of all his troubles' are rendered deeply **ironic** given the benefit of historic hindsight. The attribution of masculinity to the country is enough to alert us to the obvious point that women are oppressed and certainly not delivered from pain by men.

SELLING MANHATTAN

The title of Carol Ann Duffy's second collection signals a concern for the way in which selfish pursuit of wealth by colonists swamps and effaces culture. Although Manhattan Island is today a favoured part of New York to live for successful artists, writers, film-makers and musicians, it was originally the dwelling place of native American Indians. The Dutch settler Peter Minuit reputedly bought Manhattan from the Indians in 1626 for twenty-four dollars' worth of glass beads, a grossly exploitative act. One of the prominent themes in this collection is the way some people with a great deal of money abuse the power it spuriously confers on them. The capitalist attitude to economics is clearly criticised by the poet in 'Money Talks' and 'Selling Manhattan'. The British political climate of the 1980s is important to consider in relation to such poems. In many ways the monetarist policy of Margaret Thatcher's government paid homage to the American preference for letting the market regulate the economy. It became almost a Conservative article of faith that wealth was morally good and that 'profit is not a dirty word'. Many people, including Carol Ann Duffy, did not object to the idea of a healthy economy but questioned the reality of the increasing gap between those with a great deal of money and those with little or none. Individualism and conspicuous consumption characterised the London of the 1980s. Duffy's critique of the Conservative administration is overt in *Selling Manhattan* and becomes more pervasive in her third collection, *The Other Country*. There is a clear political dimension to this collection.

As in *Standing Female Nude* there is a notable use of the **dramatic monologue**, which gives voice to people ranging from the dispossessed to the colonist, criminal, lover, politician, psychopath, ventriloquist and servant. There are several love poems that deal with the complications and consolations of relationships. Duffy's interest in the visual arts is maintained through her triptych 'Three Paintings'.

CONTEXT

Selling Manhattan represents a clear continuation of the concerns of the previous collection; it also explores political and sexual themes that become more prominent in *The Other Country*.

MONEY TALKS

- Money is given a voice.

COMMENTARY

The title of this poem reminds us of the power of money and is accorded further weight through its **personification**. Its voice tells us that it is 'the authentic language of suffering', reminding the reader that for all those who have enough money there are many who suffer from a lack of it or are exploited terribly by those who seek riches at their expense. The emphatic use of **internal rhyme** in 'My cold, gold eye / does not blink' is a comment on the people who pursue wealth without thinking of the consequences for other people. Of course, there is also the **metaphorical image** of a gold coin being disc-shaped like an eye that does not blink.

We hear not only the voice of money but also the voices of the many that crave it, save it or desperately need it. In a sense we hear these voices refracted through the common medium of the voice of money. The prostitute who asks a customer, 'Mister, you want nice time?' highlights the power of economic necessity as well as the degrading things that people will do for money. The clearly foreign-sounding formulation achieved through the omission of the indefinite article 'a' alerts the reader to the scenario of a rich man buying the sexual services of a poor woman in a foreign country. She has learnt just enough English to sell her body. The **pun** in line 3, 'I say, *Screw You*', refers both to **slang** sexual terminology and to the unfeeling exploitative attitudes of those who only have profit as a motive. The reference to Midas reminds us that an irrational lust for money manifests itself in some people. Dionysus granted King Midas a wish and the latter asked that all he touched should turn to gold. The wish was granted and had obvious, terrible consequences; these are explored elsewhere in these Notes in connection with the poem 'Mrs Midas' from *The World's Wife*. The 'million tills' that 'sing' keep the reader in mind of the voice of money, while 'shining' and 'stink' make clear the superficial attraction of money and its negative associations. The word 'accumulate' in line 6 recalls the saying, 'You have to speculate to accumulate.' The voice of a man is foregrounded in the final line of stanza 1. It is simultaneously indicative of someone who is anxious and powerful. He has the money to pay for the good time he is providing but he doubts the authenticity of the affection of a woman who may well be taking advantage of him.

Stanza 2 deals with the all-pervasive aspect of money. There are three biblical **allusions** used reductively by Carol Ann Duffy to reinforce the arrogance of those who see wealth as being a licence to proceed as they wish in life. The first of these references is to Matthew 19:24, which asserts that 'it is easier for a camel to pass through the eye of a needle than for a rich man to enter heaven'. This emphasises the low intrinsic status attached to wealth by God and the manner in which it is so highly prized by humans. The voice of money claims to be able to do the impossible by contradicting the biblical statement: 'See me pass through the eye of a needle!' Even time can be conquered with enough money, it seems. Those who can afford a 'sleek facelift' are, of course, deluding themselves. 'Don't give me away' is **ambiguous**: it is a warning that money should not be wasted but also suggests that its secret methods of operation should not be betrayed. The statement 'I'm a jealous God' cites the words in Exodus 20:5 of the Old Testament God who visits punishment on people who do not obey him. The 'one commandment' mentioned in line 11 **ironically** reduces the Ten Commandments to just one and this is associated with money. The biblical dictum that someone 'cannot serve God and Mammon' is implicit here. The alliterative link between 'commandment' and 'calculator' intensifies Duffy's **satirical** apprehension of those who are unable to see beyond the material.

> **CONTEXT**
>
> In the New Testament of the Bible, Jesus angrily rebukes the moneylenders for being in the temple.

The primacy of the American dollar is highlighted in the stammering '$-sound' and '$-stammering' which emphasise the oral performance highlighted in the title of the poem as well as using the typographical symbol for the all-powerful American dollar. The ability to travel 'faster than sound' is yet another expression of wealth. Clearly, the poet is drawing attention to the manner in which the spiritual is being effaced by the material. The Bible commands human beings to love God with all their power and might, but money stakes a rival claim by demanding to be worshipped in this way.

The satirical **tone** of the poem is pervasive and the final stanza makes clear that ultimate power is wielded by those with most money in the form of weaponry. Behind the programmatic affability of the American courtesy phrase 'Have a good day' is the sinister reality of 'big bombs, sighing in their thick lead sheaths OK'. The final 'OK' is used by Duffy to convey the way a voice can be a disguise. The way money talks is deceitful and self-seeking.

SELLING MANHATTAN

- We hear the voice of a colonist speaking to an indigenous North American Indian who has been tricked into selling valuable tracts of land for a derisory payment.
- We hear the thoughts of an Indian reflecting upon the effects of settlement.

The voice of the greedy, arrogant, racist colonist presented in italics in stanza 1 is contrasted with the reflective, gentle voice of the Indian in the remainder of the poem.

COMMENTARY

The **irony** of '*All yours, Injun*' is striking since everything is being taken away from him for almost nothing. The colonist's selfishness is stressed in '*I got myself a bargain*', and his aggressiveness and

> **CONTEXT**
>
> Manhattan is an Amerindian word meaning 'island mountain'. The Dutch settler Peter Minuit is reputed to have bought Manhattan Island in 1626 for twenty-four dollars' worth of glass beads.

power in '*I brandish / firearms*'. The Indians gave the name 'fire-water' to whisky, something given to them by white men. This had disastrous results as their genetic make-up meant that their bodies were unable to cope with alcohol. Whisky became a real scourge. The destruction of many lives by alcohol is made more poignant by the fact that the name 'fire-water' is a typically poetic **kenning** favoured by people who also coined memorable terms such as 'iron horse' for train. The white Christian colonist cares nothing for the Indians or their culture and says '*Praise the Lord*' only because he has made a financial killing. This is made even clearer by '*Now get your red ass out of here.*'

The opening of stanza 2 contrasts sharply with the rapacious voice of the settler. The Indian wonders 'if the ground has anything to say'. The North American Indians' culture is one in which nature is revered and the concept of owning land is anathema since this would be, as far as they are concerned, like owning God. Their creation **myths** are beautiful, their people often named after creatures and place names reflect their topographical features. This man is a spokesperson for a whole people when he says, 'You have made me drunk, drowned out / the world's slow truth with rapid lies.' The obliteration of an ancient culture with all its tradition is neatly emphasised by Carol Ann Duffy in the contrasting 'slow' and 'rapid'. There is sufficient recovery from the alcoholic haze for the man to see the truth clearly and record it for posterity. In speaking in the voice of the Indian, the poet is also speaking *for* him as we remember the **artifice** involved in the **dramatic monologue**. The damning indictment of colonists all over the world is made clear in 'Wherever / you have touched the earth, the earth is sore.' This **personification** of the earth as a being capable of feeling pain is wholly consistent with the American Indians' perception of nature which, being pantheistic, signals to the reader that what has been done to their country is also an affront to their religious sensibilities. The 'starlight psalm' at the end of stanza 3 emphasises this.

> **CONTEXT**
>
> Pantheistic means believing that a divinity informs the whole of nature.

Throughout, there is a focus on the Indian's sense of connection with the earth and nature. He is keen to find out if the ground or 'the spirit of the water' has 'anything / to say', and reveres his environment, as evidenced by 'I sing with true love for the land' (line 13). He is concerned with the metaphysical aspects of life signalled through the physical, whereas the Dutch settler has only material profit in mind when he speaks of God. The Indian people's 'dawn chant, the song of sunset, starlight psalm' are a clear analogue with the Christian liturgical times of singing as set down in a book of hours, but in the case of the former they are songs specifically to those phenomena rather than prayers sung at those particular times.

Stanzas 4 and 5 are poignant in their presentation of a man speaking for a tribe. 'Trust your dreams' clearly implies that these are more reliable than dishonest colonists. The man has wisdom, gained from being in touch with the rhythms of nature, signalled by 'morning's frost and firefly's flash at night'. Duffy's use of **alliteration** links the disparate phenomena as being part of one natural system. What can be learnt in life is hard won and regulated by 'the solemn laws of joy and sorrow'. This refers in the first instance to the man's memory of the woman he loved who has now died, but his experience becomes emblematic of his tribe's. The acquisitive impulse and vanity of the colonist is further questioned when the Indian points out that short-term gain is meaningless in the face of mortality and eternity: 'how many acres do you need / to lengthen your shadow under the endless sky?' (lines 20–1). The freedom that has been taken away is movingly likened to 'the salmon going mysteriously / out to sea' (lines 23–4). The sense of cultural disorientation and disenfranchisement is memorably given weight in line 24: 'Loss holds the silence of great stones.' The massiveness and import of 'great stones' locates the man's consciousness both within his own psyche and in the collective memory of his people by associating it with the immovable stones that form the landscape. Their 'silence' is more movingly eloquent than the words of the settler in stanza 1 because their very being speaks to the indigenous population which listens to what they have to say.

QUESTION

How does Duffy write about the effects of capitalism in 'Selling Manhattan'?

The sixth stanza is one line long, suggesting a self-written epitaph by the Indian who characteristically wishes to be immortalised after his death in 'the ghost of grasshopper and buffalo'. His choice of creatures embraces the least and the greatest. The buffalo has particular cultural significance for the American Indians as it was an important source of food, was associated with rain and was the centre of several rituals. It is fitting that the line he speaks should champion his culture. It might seem that the dwindling of the American Indian presence is unstoppable and its voice isolated but the placing of this statement on a single line actually lends it great weight and significance. Typographically, it is prominent and given space between stanzas. As a statement it suggests both the seeking of solace in familiar cultural patterns and a realisation that the afterlife offers something better than the current physical situation.

The final stanza **personifies** the evening, which 'trembles and is sad' as if aware of the imminent effacement of a way of life. Strictly speaking, this is a specialised form of personification known as **pathetic fallacy**. The 'little shadow' that 'runs across the grass' symbolises, perhaps, the spirit of the Indian at death.
The fact that it is 'little' reminds us of his insignificance as far as capitalists are concerned but in the natural order something monumental has been lost. Just as he had equal reverence for the grasshopper and the buffalo, so the evening is 'sad' at his actual or prospective passing. Significantly the shadow 'disappears into the darkening pines', suggesting not annihilation but assimilation into nature.

> **CONTEXT**
>
> Pathetic fallacy is a term coined by John Ruskin in the nineteenth century to describe the way poets sometimes impose human emotion on nature for effect.

The concluding stanza could be read as narrative intervening at the end of the poem, thus making line 25 the last utterance of the Native American Indian. The expansive vision of the Indian is contrasted with the myopic self-interest of the colonist.

This poem, although concentrating on the plight of the North American Indians, could be read as a general comment on colonialism. Manhattan was named New Amsterdam in 1653 and New York City in 1664. It was another Dutchman, William of Orange, who began colonial rule of Ireland in 1690, a cultural memory very close to Carol Ann Duffy's own inheritance, making her identification with the American Indians understandably strong.

STEALING

- A burglar and petty thief talks about the items he has stolen, the most unusual of which was a snowman.

COMMENTARY

Carol Ann Duffy lived for a while by Wimbledon Common in London. Her neighbours once built a traditional snowman for their children, which was stolen. The poet wondered who might have done such a thing. She concluded that it could only have happened under the premiership of Margaret Thatcher, a period during which individualism and greed seemed to be regarded as virtues. It is clear, then, that apart from being curious about who might steal a snowman from children, Duffy regarded the actions of an individual as a barometer of the political climate. The opening of stanza 2 – 'Better off dead than giving in, not taking / what you want' – appears to encapsulate this idea.

This **dramatic monologue** is a good example of how formal organisation into stanzas of regular length can contain the informal **register** of a **persona**. Statements such as 'He weighed a ton' (line 7), 'I'm a mucky ghost' (line 13), 'I nicked a bust of Shakespeare once' (line 23) and 'flogged it' (line 24) convincingly recreate the **argot** of the man who is speaking.

He seems to derive pleasure (although this is short-lived) from gratuitous acts of burglary, enjoying the excitement or frisson of the act itself rather than really desiring the objects he steals. He leaves a 'mess' (line 13) in other people's houses. This could refer to the chaos often left behind by burglars who empty drawers and so on, but it could equally suggest defecation, a common feature of burglary. Such an act is calculated to defile victims' private places. A Freudian psychologist would suggest that its origins are sexual. There is certainly a suggestion of an auto-erotic charge in 'I watch my gloved hand twisting the doorknob. / A stranger's bedroom. Mirrors. I sigh like this – *Aah*' (lines 14–15). He also derives pleasure from speculating upon the effect that his acts will have

QUESTION

How does Duffy use the dramatic monologue in 'Stealing', 'Psychopath' (*Selling Manhattan*) and 'Havisham' (*Mean Time*)? You should consider poetic technique and the poet's treatment of themes.

on others: 'Part of the thrill was knowing / that children would cry in the morning' (lines 9–10).

The utter futility of what the man does is made clear in such details as 'I joyride cars / to nowhere' (lines 11–12). He steals a guitar but never learns to play it. Perhaps the most striking example of such futility is his attempted reassembling of the stolen snowman. His failure to recreate 'a mate' (line 3), with **connotations** of both friendship and physical intimacy, prompts him to immediate aggression and destruction, leaving him 'amongst lumps of snow, sick of the world' (line 20). This fragmentation could symbolically suggest a personality which is itself disintegrated, a **Jungian** term for describing someone who has not come to terms with his or her 'shadow'.

Duffy's use of **internal rhyme** is appropriate to the interior aspect of a dramatic monologue which seeks to explore the thief's motives for acting in the way he does. For example 'the slice of ice / within my own brain' (lines 4–5) indicates a self-awareness and concern with interior workings, which the man identifies with coldness and hardness. The second stanza's 'chill' and 'thrill' reinforce this identification. The snowman, itself a cherished object, is curiously as unfeeling as he is and conveniently 'mute' (stanza 1).

> **CONTEXT**
>
> 'Stealing' is another of Duffy's explorations of the minds of those who are mentally unstable. Useful comparisons are 'Psychopath' (*Selling Manhattan*), 'Liar' (*The Other Country*) and 'Havisham' (*Mean Time*).

THE VIRGIN PUNISHING THE INFANT

- Three men, looking through a window, see a mother spanking her child.
- The poem is written in the collective voice of a small village community reflecting on the effect the infant Jesus's claim to being divine has on his mother, and on them.

This poem was inspired by the painting by the **surrealist** Max Ernst (1891–1976), *The Virgin Punishing the Infant*. Unlike the conventional presentation of the Madonna and child, we see the mother spanking the baby. His halo has fallen off and lies forlornly in the corner of the room. This clearly signifies the ordinariness of the situation but, like the poem, leaves some possibility of power. The halo, or nimbus, is a familiar and traditional **symbol** of holiness in paintings of the saints and the Holy Family.

COMMENTARY

Joseph, the carpenter, is presented as a 'simple man' who had not bargained for being the foster father of the Almighty. The picture painted of him 'carving himself / a silent Pinocchio out in the workshed' (lines 2–3) gives an amusing insight into a person who wished for a son but feels he has to create him in his own image, through a means with which he is familiar. This might seem like an odd way of setting about creating a son but for the fact that Joseph had to accept that the woman to whom he was betrothed had conceived a child by the power of God. The village is **personified** as it 'gossiped in the sun' (line 7), indicating its inhabitants are oblivious to the significance of the son in their midst. They see him as an oddity and embarrassment to his mother, a prodigy who is liable to cause his parents sorrow. He will, of course, himself become the man of sorrows (Isaiah 53:3). The weight of the world's sin is hardly insignificant.

The predicament of Mary is presented in straightforward practical terms. The conclusion, in contrast to the remainder of the poem, allows for the possibility of the child actually being divine: 'But afterwards, we wondered / why the infant did not cry. And why the Mother did.' Mary could well be weeping because she is aware of the terrible experience her little son will suffer as a crucified man.

CHECK THE NET

Search the Internet for an image of Max Ernst's *The Virgin Punishing the Infant.*

WARMING HER PEARLS

- A young maid wears her mistress's necklace in order that her body heat will add lustre to the pearls.
- This leads her to reflect upon her love for the woman.

This **dramatic monologue** explores the sexual feelings of one woman for another as she handles a string of pearls belonging to

CONTEXT

Domestic servants were widely employed by middle-class families well into the first half of the twentieth century. The aristocracy still has servants.

CONTEXT

In its exploration of the homoerotic, 'Warming Her Pearls' anticipates some of the poems in *The Other Country*.

CONTEXT

The word *stanza* is Italian for 'room', and it is fitting that the similar dimensions of Duffy's stanzas should also draw attention to the very different emotional and societal situations of these women.

her. Thus the boundaries of class and **stereotypical** sexual identity are being crossed.

COMMENTARY

It was common practice for maids to warm the pearls of their mistresses, and this information forms the starting point of the poem. The pearls become for the maid emblematic of her mistress. When she says in the final stanza 'All night / I feel their absence and I burn' she is really feeling the absence of the woman she has just visualised 'Slipping naked into bed' (stanza 5).

The maid is acutely aware of her mistress's body as she is obviously in daily, intimate contact with her despite the class difference and clearly defined working relationship. The precise visual details of 'cool white throat' and 'slim hand' indicate how closely she observes her body while 'the Yellow Room' signals a familiarity with the geography of the house. The maid can only 'dream' about the mistress from a distance in her 'attic bed', but the intimacy she craves, made plain in 'my red lips part', has been realised in some measure as she has worn the pearls. The erotic charge of 'my slow heat entering / each pearl' is clear. Similarly, the maid imagining her mistress being perplexed by her own 'persistent scent / beneath her French perfume' indicates physical intimacy.

The obsession of the maid for her mistress is agonising for her and she imagines 'her every movement'. The use of **ellipsis** in the final two stanzas indicates first the way in which she visualises the mistress's taking her clothes off as being highly significant, '… Undressing', and then the way time seems to slow down as she thinks of her in her bed: '… And I lie here awake'. The pearls 'cooling' and the aching sense of their 'absence' make her 'burn' with passion.

The poet's use of **enjambment** is particularly skilful at the end of stanza 5 as the mistress in her bed and the maid in hers are linked through the latter's familiarity with her employer's most intimate habits. Typographically, the stanzas are separated like the rooms occupied by the women.

THE OTHER COUNTRY

In this, her third collection, Carol Ann Duffy continues to explore personal and social themes alongside political concerns. She **satirises** the gratuitous factionalism of politicians, and the gross offensiveness of the tabloid press. In the face of such forces she also reminds us of the power of truth and love. *The Other Country*, like *Mean Time*, overtly explores the possibilities and limitations of language.

The title of the collection is highly significant and, in common with her other volumes, both deliberately **ambiguous** and yet curiously definitive. It acts as a cohering force, bringing a range of issues in one's own country into sharp focus while simultaneously suggesting that the 'other country' might be a preferable place to inhabit. There is a suggestion that we are experiencing the perspectives of another country from within the country itself. There is equally a sense that there is another country beyond the one with which we are immediately familiar. This collection is perhaps more overtly concerned with the politics of Britain than either *Standing Female Nude* or *Selling Manhattan*. In particular, Duffy addresses the years during which Margaret Thatcher was prime minister. Several poems in *The Other Country* articulate anger and frustration at what amounts to the transformation of Britain into a country that is almost unrecognisable as compared to the one people were used to. On another level we are certainly led to reflect on the geographical differences between countries and the effects these have. For example, language, distance and difference all have a part to play in our interpretation of the title's significations.

 QUESTION

One of Duffy's major concerns in *The Other Country* is the way Britain changed during the 1980s. Choose two poems from this collection and write about the ways in which she makes this concern evident.

It is difficult not to hear the resonance of L. P. Hartley's famous opening sentence in his novel *The Go-Between* (1953): 'The past is a foreign country: they do things differently there'. This is certainly one of the other countries Duffy explores – the land of childhood and memory. Also, we might hear echoes of Hamlet's words concerning death, 'The undiscovered country, from whose bourn / No traveller returns' (*Hamlet*, III.1.79–80). Death is confronted in a number of poems in this collection. The idea of platonic, sexual or romantic love as being another country is also examined. Indeed, another person's otherness can, in a very striking sense, make them seem like an unexplored country.

It is wholly fitting that even the title of this collection offers a plurality of meanings since a poet is primarily concerned with such potential in language, and readers are not led to seek a single, reductive 'answer' while engaging in the business of interpretation.

ORIGINALLY

- The opening poem in the collection introduces ideas about another country as well as exploring some of the more metaphorical implications of otherness.
- The poem tells of a family moving house with all the attendant changes and anxieties a child might experience.

CONTEXT

In this poem Duffy writes from a dual perspective – as the adult who was once a child and as the child who would later become an adult.

COMMENTARY

The plural possessive pronoun 'We' that begins the poem signals a collective family identity. It recaptures the child's identification of experience as something defined within the parameters of a familiar, known social unit. The child remembers the car they travelled in as a 'red room' which 'fell through the fields'. The emotional wrench of moving house as a child is clearly presented in the brothers crying and one 'bawling *Home, / Home*'. The noisy chaos of such a scene is economically recreated and the pull of the family home is conveyed through Duffy's mental retracing of the route the family has taken back to 'the city, / the street, the house, the vacant rooms / where we didn't live any more' (lines 5–7). This is easily identified with as children very often have a sense of self, place and others that we might see as concentric. In James Joyce's *A Portrait of the Artist as a Young Man* (1915), Stephen Daedalus writes in the flyleaf of his geography book:

Stephen Daedalus
Class of Elements
Clongowes Wood College
Sallins
County Kildare
Ireland
Europe
The world
The universe.

Like James Joyce's novel, this poem is certainly largely autobiographical. The child 'stared / at the eyes of a blind toy, holding its paw', demonstrating a need for comfort at such a time of distress but reminding the reader that her adult poet-self now observes that the toy could neither see or feel. This makes a situation from the past more moving for the reader as it emphasises the child's emotional needs.

We have been explicitly told that the family moved from one country to another. In the opening of stanza 2, 'All childhood is an emigration', there are both literal and **metaphorical** dimensions to consider. We already know that a childhood emigration has occurred but the idea of childhood as emigration reflects upon the magnitude of change involved as we grow towards adulthood. Such growth may be 'slow' or 'sudden'. It is the traumatic interruption of the 'slow' process that Carol Ann Duffy focuses on. Being catapulted into a new set of social and cultural circumstances is finely drawn in such terms as 'Your accent wrong' (line 12), 'unimagined pebble-dashed estates' (line 13) and 'words you don't understand' (line 14). The child feels displaced and unable to make any adjustment in this other country. Things may 'seem familiar' but they are made foreign because of her difference. The vulnerability of the little girl is made clear through the reference to 'big boys' who ate worms and yelled obscenities. The poet's adult self is able to see that her parents were worried about the effect of the move on their children: 'My parents' anxiety stirred like a loose tooth / in my head'. The choice of **simile** identifies the experience in terms of a familiar physiological change in a child but also stresses the psychological implications as she faces change in every sense.

> **CONTEXT**
>
> Duffy's family did move from Scotland to England.

QUESTION

Choose another poem to compare with 'Originally' that deals with the theme of childhood and/or identity.

The use of italics in the last line of the stanza dramatises the child's sense of self and place in a simple and touching cry from the heart: '*I want our own country*, I said'. This, by extension, invites us to consider our childhood past as another or foreign country where things were indeed done differently.

The final stanza reflects upon how our natural survival mechanisms tend to take over: 'But then you forget, or don't recall, or change' (line 17). The child who was so exposed and vulnerable feels only 'a skelf of shame' as her brother swallows a slug. The children have become part of another country and culture. Duffy deftly shows the children being assimilated into the new way of life by describing an awareness of betraying the old one by using the **dialect** word 'skelf', which is a splinter. The capitulation seems to be complete with the poet's adaptation of her accent for the purpose of gaining social acceptance. In linguistic terms she has accommodated the accent of others. She likens this change to a snake 'shedding its skin', indicating a new exterior with the self remaining intact. We might say, then, that Carol Ann Duffy presents us with a dual idea of betrayal. In the first place the children 'betray' their difference simply by opening their mouths and behaving according to their own customs, but later they betray their own culture by taking to the ways of the 'other country'.

These memories move the poet to reflect upon their significance and those things we tend to identify as defining our sense of self and community. She asks herself whether she 'only' lost things identifiable in geographical, linguistic or sociological terms, and part of the answer must surely be that in losing them she may sometimes feel that she lost part of herself and a sense of who she really is. This is neatly summarised at the end of the poem as Duffy reminds us that early displacement can lead us to find it difficult to identify precisely where we come from. We 'hesitate' when quizzed about our origins.

The relationship between the past and the present is clearly conveyed in 'Originally' and there is a strong sense that one is very much a product of one's past. This is a poem about childhood, memory, roots, and identity.

IN MRS TILSCHER'S CLASS

- The remembered security of Mrs Tilscher's primary-school class is contrasted with the uncertainties attached to growing towards adolescence, starting secondary school, and dealing with the horror of the Moors Murders.

COMMENTARY

The first two stanzas concentrate upon the wonder felt by the child as she discovers the world through sight, sound, smell, touch, hearing and taste. The security of a childhood idyll is captured in the accumulation of details. The geography lesson that begins the day transports the children to another country through the use of a map, which they can see and touch. They hear Mrs Tilscher, who 'chanted the scenery' (line 3). The details of school experience are couched in terms of a child's perception. For example, at break time the children drink 'a skittle of milk', and the 'Pyramids' learnt about in the morning lesson are recalled imaginatively through the concrete **image** of the last remnant of a stick of chalk 'rubbed into dust'. The carefree aspect of childhood is conveyed in the joyous sentence: 'The laugh of a bell swung by a running child' (line 8). The **personification** of the bell transfers the exuberance of the energetic child to the thing he or she is required to ring.

The school environment is perceived by the child as being 'better than home', a place where news of the Moors Murderers 'faded, like the faint, uneasy smudge of a mistake' (line 12). This contemporary reference is to Ian Brady and Myra Hindley, who horrifically tortured and murdered two children on Saddleworth Moor in Lancashire in 1965 (see 'The Devil's Wife', *The World's Wife*). The anxiety of news from a dangerous world outside is effaced like a mistake rubbed out by the child. The truth that emerges by the end of the poem, though, is that the unpalatable, difficult areas of life cannot be so easily effaced. Even the eraser leaves a 'faint, uneasy smudge' indicating that the trace of something, once there, cannot be obliterated. The stanza closes with references to the promotion of self-worth through the reward system of 'good gold'

CONTEXT

The use of the senses is a striking feature of this poem. It is appropriate that sensory experience should predominate, since this is very much at the centre of how young children learn best, and influences the way primary schools organise the curriculum.

stars and the characteristically evocative smells and sounds of the primary-school classroom. The maternal, committed and benign presence of Mrs Tilscher is reflected in the way she 'loved you' and 'slowly, carefully' shaved a pencil. This place is not the locus of disaffection catalogued in some of the poems about secondary school in *Standing Female Nude* but shows children eager to learn, in a classroom seen as being as attractive as a sweet shop. That this phase of education is something still very much characterised by the formative process of discovery is emphasised by the 'xylophone's nonsense heard from another form'. The younger children are making tentative, uninhibited moves towards learning music.

The third and fourth stanzas explore the changed child, the one who is now at the stage where he or she is not really a child and not quite an adolescent. The 'Easter term' in stanza 3 heralds the imminent move to a new school as well as reminding us of a seasonal shift into spring with all its possibilities associated with growth and new life. The release of frogs 'by a dunce' into the playground is presented humorously, with children 'croaking' after them in a lunch queue, but there is a more sinister dimension to be considered. The life cycle of the frogs is referred to in the striking visual image of 'the inky tadpoles changed / from commas into exclamation marks'. These ink and punctuation marks are familiar details in the classroom, as are the tadpoles, but Duffy is also referring to the metamorphosis of the child into the pre-adolescent. In much the same way that Seamus Heaney signals the invasion of childhood experience in the second part of his 1966 poem 'Death of a Naturalist' with the lines:

> Then one hot day when fields were rank
> With cowdung in the grass the angry frogs
> Invaded the flax-dam

Duffy presents a 'rough boy' revealing the sexual truth of her biological origins. The truth is resisted temporarily, literally 'kicked' against in the form of the boy, but a threshold has been crossed; there is no going back to the country of childhood.

QUESTION

Look carefully at Duffy's use of imagery in this poem and the way in which it reflects the child **persona** in the poem.

QUESTION

How does Duffy use imagery and stanzaic structure in 'In Mrs Tilscher's Class'?

The final stanza is characterised by images associated with suppressed passion, impatience and sexuality. The school year is at its end and Duffy uses the imminent storm to convey the dual sense of excitement and danger associated with the self-discovery of the emergent adolescent. The air which 'tasted of electricity' captures this very effectively while the adjectives 'feverish', 'hot' and 'sexy' stress incipient sexuality. The change in the weather, which erupts into a storm, presages the stormy time of adolescence. There is a clear sense of a rite of passage being gone through as the children 'ran through the gates' of the school 'impatient to be grown'.

Like 'Originally', this is a poem about change. Just as William Blake did, Duffy presents the transformation of childhood innocence into adult experience. In terms of the title of the collection in which it appears, it charts part of the process of 'emigration' from the country of childhood to that of the adult. Put in stronger terms, we might say that we witness the invasion of innocence by experience, terms appropriate to the **metaphorical** concept of separate countries.

WEASEL WORDS

- A group of weasels teach another group of animals, the ferrets, about the inability of their opponents to tell the truth.

In this **sonnet**, Carol Ann Duffy humorously examines the duplicity and dishonesty of politicians. Their factionalism is clearly presented through the use of animals as a typifying factor. It is redolent of the weasels and stoats in Kenneth Grahame's *The Wind in the Willows* (1908). The occasion that prompted the poem's composition is clearly stated in the introductory remarks about Sir Robert Armstrong. The term 'weasel words' became assimilated into the common parlance of political commentators.

CONTEXT

'Which is more than can be said for the Ferrets opposite' (line 9): in the House of Commons, site of political debate in Britain (Scotland now has its own parliament), the party forming the government faces the opposition across the floor of the house.

www. **CHECK THE NET**

To look at Hansard, the official record of parliamentary debates, search **http://www. parliament.the- stationery- office.co.uk**

COMMENTARY

One of the poem's themes is the way politicians use language dishonestly and hypocritically. It also shows the manner in which opposing factions almost invariably disagree with and denigrate one another. The techniques employed in the House of Commons can seem very juvenile at times with politicians trying to score points. The structure of the sonnet reflects the apparently logical progress of a political speech. The control over language, which characterises a sonnet, usually makes us aware of the skill of the poet. In this case Duffy highlights the politician's facility with language only to remind us that the egg he uses as a concrete visual aid is sucked dry, becoming as hollow and empty as his words. Just as the politician appropriates language for his own purposes, the poet chooses the sonnet form as part of her **ironic** purpose to draw attention to the hijacking of a traditional **lyric** form.

The italicised words such as '*Weasel laughter*' remind us that Duffy has Hansard in mind, the official written, verbatim record of all parliamentary proceedings. The writers of this publication are required to record all that occurs. So, if a group of politicians from a particular party shouted abuse at an opponent, this would have to be written into the official record.

PÈRE LACHAISE

* The poet muses upon the lives of the dead writers, musicians and artists buried in Père Lachaise, the famous cemetery in Paris.

Keeping the idea of another country in mind, we might remember the words of Hamlet referred to in the introductory remarks about this collection. The poet contrasts the living and the dead. The living come to think quietly about the great creative geniuses entombed in the cemetery. This contrast is made more explicit in the symbolic counterpointing of the springtime with past deaths of those remembered in the poem.

COMMENTARY

The 'breathing trees' are contrasted with the 'thousand lost talents' that are now 'dust'. The poet is brought up short by the stark reality of mortality and opens the fourth stanza with the bald sentence 'Forever dead.' This is enough to 'dizzy' her and us. There is no sense here that there is life beyond death as might be expected in a Christian cemetery. Duffy cannot subscribe to this idea and sees immortality in terms of the preservation of the dead in the memories of the living. This makes clear the importance of 'Do not forget' (line 8). The recitation of the 'sad tourists' also keeps them alive beyond the grave, 'titles of poems, paintings, songs'.

The 'white flags' (line 6) suggest the traditional **symbol** of surrender in wartime. Here, though, Duffy seems to be suggesting that even though death may have taken the physicality of dead artists away, their spirit is everlasting in the memory. The inclusion of Proust in the list of writers is particularly significant since his novel *À la Recherche du Temps Perdu* (*Remembrance of Things Past*) is, like the cemetery, concerned with commemoration. Many of the people mentioned were in the vanguard of the Aesthetic and modernist movements at the end of the nineteenth century and the early part of the twentieth century. The defiance of Edith Piaf and her contempt for convention encapsulated in her song '*Je ne regrette rien*' live on in the image of the two young men who 'embrace' near her tomb.

Another significant point here is that the dead have the power to move the living because they have become immortalised through their work.

WORDS, WIDE NIGHT

- Someone speaks to a lover in her mind across the distance of night.

COMMENTARY

The first stanza creates a reflective, languid mood. The earth's rotation and its effects are subtly presented in the description of the

CONTEXT

The distance between what we feel and our capacity to articulate such feeling is explored in this poem.

CHECK THE BOOK

Ludwig Wittgenstein's *Tractatus Logico-Philosophicus*, translated by C. K. Ogden (1981), was one of the texts Duffy studied as an undergraduate.

room 'turning slowly away from the moon'. The act of remembering the lover is 'pleasurable'. The lover who is in the mind of the poet is a long way away. The physical distance between them and the resultant longing is expressed in terms of an awareness of the limitations of language: 'In one of the tenses I singing / an impossible song of desire that you cannot hear'. This is a provocative and potentially difficult construction but it seems that Duffy is deliberately using an 'impossible tense' in order to present the idea that she is trying to articulate that which is, ultimately, inarticulable.

The impossible tense reminds us that there are things that are unthinkable, since the limits of language are the limits of thought. Wittgenstein's remark 'Unsayable things do indeed exist' is itself something that, tautologically, cannot be said or thought. His famous statement 'Whereof one cannot speak thereof one must be silent' appears to be intimately linked with the problem Duffy deftly articulates in this poem. It is a metaphysical statement that attempts to convey the unsayable, unthinkable contention that there is a dimension about which we can say nothing. It seems, though, that the limits of language are not contingent with the limits of feeling, something that Duffy seeks to address.

RIVER

- The poet reflects upon the physical attributes of a river and the metaphorical associations it has with language.

In common with several poems in *Mean Time*, the collection following *The Other Country*, Carol Ann Duffy reflects upon the possibilities of language. The only means at her disposal is to use words, the things that the critic Terry Eagleton calls 'the common counters of experience'.

COMMENTARY

Although a river may cross physical borders and barriers, it is not limited by the constraints of different languages in doing so;

it 'translates itself'. In contrast 'words stumble', the hard consonant 'b' emphasising the clumsiness that can accompany translation. The bird that the woman tries to name in stanza 2 is the same irrespective of the language of the person naming it. The physical act of preserving the flower, which is pressed 'carefully between the pages of a book', is an interesting way of showing how such an action following the purely sensory experience of a 'red flower' can be relived independent of language. The fact that it is pressed between pages of words is a striking reminder that there is more than one way to preserve memories.

The question posed to the reader at the beginning of stanza 3 again invites us to concentrate on the actual experience of things rather than worrying too much about what name to give them. We are able to derive 'meanings' from sensory detail in a much more direct way. Language is, after all, a code we use to articulate that very experience and, as such, could be seen to have secondary importance outside the normal need to communicate with others. There is, though, the residual problem that we think almost exclusively with reference to linguistic structures. The **image** of the 'blue and silver fish' that 'dart away over stone, / stoon, stein, like the meanings of things' reiterates the idea that meaning is elusive and language is protean. The signifying system we use in one language is different in another but they all mean essentially the same thing. The proximity of spelling of 'stone' in three languages and the resulting **alliteration** emphasise the poet's point.

As well as highlighting the difficulty presented by language, Duffy is careful to stress the possibilities offered by words. They are able, for example, to make the woman feel she is 'somewhere else'. Her language-framed thoughts are able to transport her and make her feel good.

 QUESTION

Compare 'River' and 'Words, Wide Night', paying close attention to the ways in which Duffy explores both the limits and possibilities of language.

The concluding lines of the poem challenge the reader with another question. The idea of writing a postcard is connected with brevity and, often, writing from a new place or country in a way that tells another person something about it. The whole problem of the relationship between experience and articulation is wonderfully presented in the image of an estuary, a place where a river becomes 'translated' into sea.

As an ultimate **symbol** of flux and change, a river is an ideal **metaphor** for Duffy's exploration of the way language changes and the way in which it relates to landscape.

Heraclitus, the fifth-century BC Presocratic Greek philosopher, wrote that 'You cannot step twice into the same river', indicating that nothing stays the same. The link between this and the theme of change in *The Other Country* is an important one as it acknowledges that a good deal is beyond the control of the individual.

MEAN TIME

CHECK THE BOOK

Michael Schmidt's *Lives of the Poets* (1998) is an accessible study of poets through the centuries that helps to place Duffy and her contemporaries in context.

In many respects, *Mean Time* is the bleakest of Carol Ann Duffy's collections. There is an atmosphere of gloom in several poems that focus on the effects of damaged or irreconcilable relationships. The political climate, as well as the personal contexts investigated, gives little room for optimism. There are frequent attempts to salvage consolation from a cosmos that seems to have set its face flint-like against humanity. Memory often offers temporary respite from the harsh realities that must be faced in the present, but even these are not always helpful.

There are various significations in the title of the collection. Time can be 'mean' in the sense that it is malevolent. In this case we may view the title as a rather negative **personification** of time. We refer to doing something 'in the mean time' which suggests that we are waiting for something more significant to happen. Another interpretation is based on the fact that 'mean' also refers to average. Time, in a sense, averages out our experience by framing our existence within a continuum that finally reduces each of us to nothing more than a brief interruption in the world. We are familiar with Greenwich Mean Time, a precise measurement of time from which bearings may be taken. We set our clocks by GMT, on the whole, and we may easily view this as a reminder that we are unable to escape the tyranny of time. The slippage that results in our losing time when the clocks go forward or back is explored in the poem 'Mean Time'. In fact, we find it virtually impossible to utter anything that does not somehow make reference to time. Almost all sentences we write or speak contain verbs indicating whether we are referring to past, present or future.

THE CAPTAIN OF THE 1964 *TOP OF THE FORM* TEAM

- We hear the voice of a man who has never got over the disappointment of growing up.
- He hankers for the time in the 1960s when he was living the uncomplicated life of a schoolboy at the top of his class and captain of a quiz team.

CONTEXT

The poem is very evocative of the 1960s with its many contemporary references.

This opening poem in the collection explores the manner in which time can be 'mean' in the sense of inflicting emotional pain. As the man grows older, his horizons have not really expanded. His younger self becomes a straitjacket on his adult life, which has signalled decline rather than progression or development. Although physically older and a husband with a wife and children, he cannot really deal with arriving in what amounts to the separate country of adult life with all its complications, disappointments and uncertainties. There are no 'correct' answers any more.

CONTEXT

Top of the Form was a popular radio general knowledge quiz, the junior equivalent of *University Challenge*.

COMMENTARY

The poem opens with the speaker of this **dramatic monologue** recalling the titles of popular songs. They help to fix the year 1964 in his mind. This is a familiar thought process as many people identify specific years in their lives with the release of records. Even the month of the releases is imprinted in his memory as it is associated with the special event of appearing on a quiz show.

CONTEXT

'Do Wah Diddy Diddy', 'Baby Love' and 'Oh Pretty Woman' are songs by Manfred Mann, The Supremes and Roy Orbison respectively.

The 1960s were a time of great national optimism following the post-war years of austerity in the 1950s. It was during this decade that the then British prime minister, Harold Macmillan, told people that they had 'never had it so good', and the American president, John F. Kennedy, announced that men would set foot on the moon

CONTEXT

Vimto is a fruit cordial.

before the end of the decade. In this context, it is not difficult to appreciate that the natural 'fizzing hope' of the boy in stanza 1 can be equated with the general mood of the time. Duffy clearly links the **onomatopoeic** 'fizzing' to such optimism. In using the word 'Gargling' she employs the same poetic technique as well as indicating boyish lack of inhibition. The boy's satchel has a 'clever smell' he associates with his past sense of self-belief. His emergent sexuality is economically alluded to in his reference to 'Convent girls' (line 6). The stanza finishes with an image of an adolescent emulating Mick Jagger's use of a steel comb as a musical instrument and relaying the physical effect of this on his lips which, in the **demotic argot** of the time, are described as being 'numb as a two-hour snog'.

CONTEXT

Mick Jagger (1943–) is an English pop musician, the singer for the Rolling Stones.

The second stanza of the poem presents the **persona** rehearsing some of the facts that once made him so successful. The first sentence – 'No snags' – contrasts with later complications and disappointments catalogued in the final stanza. The facts about the Nile and the hummingbird are cast in the present tense. This is significant because the man is trying to make his past become his present. The italicised words are light sound bites of the man's young voice when he was invariably '*Correct*'. The boy 'sped down Dyke Hill' on his bicycle, imagining himself as a cowboy on a horse. The word 'whooped' reminds the reader again that the boy was imitating an idol of popular culture, this time from film. The confident riding of the bicycle/horse with 'no hands' signals a naive lack of foresight that is characteristic of youth. The child feels on top of the world but is **ironically** speeding down a hill unable to avoid what will become a decline into his middle years. Duffy deftly signals such a transition in the movement from stanza 2 to 3.

CONTEXT

Dave Dee, Dozy, Beaky, Mick and Tich were the members of a UK male vocal band who had hits in the British charts between 1965 and 1969.

The boy declines a Latin verb, which modulates into the name of a pop group. This is done through what amounts to poetic sleight of sound. The use of **alliteration** unifies the academic 'learning' of Latin with the absorption of popular culture through sound identity. Also, the two areas of work and recreation are undifferentiated in the boy's mind but will become increasingly separated as he grows older. Although there are serious elements to consider here, the basic effect of this transition is humorous (audiences hearing Carol Ann Duffy read the poem invariably laugh at this point).

Stanza 3 continues to emphasise that the man can only preserve the cherished past in his memory and this serves to reinforce the pain of its loss. He remembers his mother keeping mementoes of his success such as his 'mascot Gonk' and a photograph of him in his *Top of the Form* team. The detailed references to clothing allow him to reinvest himself in past time. The fact that he recalls the 'first chord' of the Beatles song *A Hard Day's Night* is both evocative for any reader who knew the song in its original context and representative of the man's earlier sense of beginnings. He defines himself in terms of the time he once lived in and not that in which he lives now. The recreation of the geography of his childhood environment is also important in Duffy's presentation of the man in question. The child's familiarity with his environment is reflected in 'the Spinney' (a northern term for a wood), Churchill Way, Nelson Drive. As in so many towns, there are roads named after famous people but there is a sense here that the boy is blissfully unaware that anyone could be more 'famous' (stanza 2) than he is. Such simplicity is reinforced by the references to 'pink pavements' and 'a blue evening' which not only evoke carefree summer games of childhood but suggest an uncomplicated, **stereotyped** colour association of pink and hopscotch with girls, and animal pawprints on the soles of shoes with boys. He refers to the past as 'My country' (line 24). This sentence sums up what he feels about the past and something he tries to reclaim in his constant quizzing of a 'stale wife' and 'thick kids' (stanza 4). The sentence is repeated in the final line of the poem ahead of '*How many florins in a pound?*' This italicised question, along with the others in the final stanza, clearly suggests that he asks members of his family the answers to them but it is equally apparent that some are those he was asked as captain of the *Top of the Form* team.

The most important question posed, '*How can we know the dancer from the dance?*', and one the persona is only able to repeat rather than answer, is a quotation from W. B. Yeats's 1927 poem 'Among School Children'. In fact it is the final sentence of that poem. In it, Yeats writes about the experience of visiting a convent school where children are taught 'to be neat in everything'. He muses on himself as being 'A sixty-year-old smiling public man'. However, his public persona is at odds with his memory, which drifts back to his past

CONTEXT

Gonk is a grotesque-looking toy with shocking-coloured hair. Gonks were popular in the 1960s and early 1970s, often appearing as good-luck mascots in quiz shows.

CONTEXT

A *Hard Day's Night* was a hit record and 1964 film by The Beatles.

CONTEXT

Dusty Springfield (1939–99) was an English pop singer, particularly successful in the 1960s.

CONTEXT

'*the Prime Minister of Rhodesia*' refers to Ian Smith (1919–), who was well known for his insistence on independence for that country (now Zimbabwe).

CONTEXT

A florin was a pre-decimal coin worth two shillings, the equivalent of ten new pence.

and a time when he was himself full of possibilities as a young man in love with the beautiful Maud Gonne. The second stanza reflects upon being told a story by Gonne about something 'trivial / That changed some childish day to tragedy'. He imagines his lover as a child of an age with those he is currently visiting. In this respect the wistful sense of loss is paralleled in the quiz captain's musing about his lost past. Another possible connection to be made is that the man can only really feel at home in a recreated past populated by schoolchildren. Yeats's question also asks us to consider the relationship between the artist and the work of art. A deconstructive critic might suggest that the question is not a rhetorical one and that in repeating this the speaker in the poem is drawing attention to the unstable relationship between **sign** and **signified**, something that echoes his unstable relationship with the world around him. The man presented in the poem attempts to create reality from a construct but can only fail to recapture what is gone. We are also reminded here of Marcel Proust (1871–1922), the French novelist whose *À la Recherche du Temps Perdu* (literally *In Search of Lost Time*) sums up what the persona tries to do. Proust's title is often translated as *Remembrance of Things Past* but this fails to capture the **pathos** of the original French. Indeed, the effects of lost time and loss caused by the passage of time are ideas Duffy returns to in several poems in this collection. The invasion of the world of the child by that of the adult is chillingly alluded to: 'I smiled / as wide as a child who went missing on the way home / from school' (stanza 4). The photographs of abducted children are inevitably happy portraits, intensifying the impact of their abduction by predatory adults. The presentation of this unpalatable reality is reminiscent of the reference to 'Brady and Hindley' in stanza 2 of 'In Mrs Tilscher's Class' from *The Other Country*.

CONTEXT

The references to popular culture and the allusiveness of this poem make it one that repays careful reading.

Despite its lightness of **tone** and humorous touches, this opening poem takes up some of the serious ideas in Carol Ann Duffy's previous collection, and introduces the themes of childhood, memory and time key in this one. The second stanza of 'Originally' from *The Other Country* asserts that 'All childhood is an emigration.' The man in this poem has, **metaphorically**, become a refugee from the past, which is, as L. P. Hartley (1895–1972) in his novel *The Go-Between* says, 'a foreign country'.

LITANY

- A group of women, including the poet's mother, sit in a neighbour's living room looking at items they have bought from a catalogue or at pictures of things they might like to buy.
- The child embarrasses her mother by recounting the way a boy at school told her to 'fuck off'.
- Her punishment is to be made to wash her mouth out with soap.

The child in this poem is cast in the dual role of observer and social saboteur. Through the power of language she shames her mother by using an obscenity in front of her assembled friends. The poem itself is a means of championing the power of words in that it is able to articulate a great deal about the women who found language so difficult to deal with.

This poem looks at the way working-class attitudes to life can be stultifying. It also shows how a child develops a clear sense of his or her own identity. The dangers of school are highlighted in that parents have no real control over the influences their children are likely to encounter outside the family context. It also reminds us of the delicious power words are able to wield but also that language itself can be very shocking and hurtful to those in authority; it can challenge that authority and the values enshrined in a family or society.

 QUESTION

How does Duffy present attitudes to language in this poem in terms of its social, religious and generational uses?

COMMENTARY

The presentation of the women is largely negative. They seem limited, conventional and uncompromising. Their horizons extend only to what is contained in catalogues. Their conversations clearly centre on fashion and other small talk in each other's houses over tea and biscuits. The opening of the poem recalls the women's conversation as a 'soundtrack'; it formed the background to childhood experience like the soundtrack or dialogue of a film. A 'litany' is a list and it tends to be associated with prayer. In the

CONTEXT

A sequence of
stanzas may
have the same
dimensions in
terms of the
number and
length of lines,
but will vary in
the **images** and
diction employed.

Catholic Church, the litany of saints is a well-known prayer. This idea clearly renders the recitation '*candlewick / bedspread three-piece suite display cabinet*' **ironic** in that it is a secularisation of the term. There is no punctuation separating the items on the list, suggesting a mindless subscription to a way of life that can accept these things along with '*Pyrex*', 'cellophane' and 'polyester shirts'.

The women are described as 'stiff-haired', suggesting that they are uncompromising. They have 'terrible marriages', which are **metaphorically** presented as 'cellophane / round polyester shirts'; both the wrapping and the contents are artificial, synthetic. Duffy compounds this sense of artificiality by observing that social equilibrium is precarious – the wives 'balanced' their 'red smiles' which were, of course, garishly accentuated with lipstick. Even Mrs Barr's leg is encased in nylon stockings, the fashionable shade of which was 'American Tan'. The 'ladder' in her tights is described through a **simile** by the poet as being 'sly / like a rumour', showing how something that starts out as being apparently innocuous can develop into something more serious and damaging. The women's eyes, 'hard / as the bright stones in engagement rings', caused the lounge to 'bristle'. These details, along with their 'sharp hands', suggest that they are brittle like the '*Pyrex*' they cook with. The word 'poised' helps to recreate the visual dimension of a familiar scene in which a group of friends reach a hiatus in a conversation when something 'embarrassing' is broached. The words that signify these things such as 'sex' and 'cancer' are taboo subjects even now for some people. The embarrassment was dealt with by spelling out words letter by letter. This was a means of defusing what were clearly perceived as linguistic bombs. The response to the child's reported '*fuck off*' is enough to convey this. Duffy seamlessly modulates from 'biscuits' to a word 'broken / to bits', using both **alliteration** and **enjambment** to make clear the idea of fracturing in the process of spelling it out. The profusion of hard consonants that predominate in the words associated with the women helps to create the mood that prepares the reader for their unsympathetic 'uproar'. The tension built up through several of the words already quoted is heightened by the simile 'tensed the air like an accident'. Such tension is temporarily relieved in the remainder of the stanza. Humorous observation indicates that the women's wilfulness in refusing to acknowledge the reality of 'cancer, or sex, or debts' is only matched by their ignorance, 'and certainly not leukaemia, which no one could spell'. The third stanza finishes with images of death and discovery. The child remembers the time of year at the end of a long summer which, by a metaphor, she calls 'a mass grave of wasps'. They, like the women, lost their sting and capacity to scare. They 'bobbed' harmlessly in a 'jam jar'. The final line of the stanza shifts to the **image** of a butterfly which 'stammered itself' in the child's 'curious hands'. The physical sensation of a butterfly fluttering in one's hands is skilfully evoked here and the choice of verb is doubly effective as it draws attention to a term we use to describe someone struggling (often nervously) to articulate what it is they wish to say. It symbolically represents the child's search for identity through voice. Children are, of course, naturally curious, as much about how far they are able to push their parents as about the verities of existence. A butterfly as **symbol** of freedom and change is also important; it emerges from the chrysalis and takes flight. It is clear that one should be careful not to expect a single 'equivalent meaning' for images a poet employs.

QUESTION

Choose at least two more of Duffy's poems about childhood experience and compare them closely with 'Litany'.

Any nervousness implied by the word 'stammered' in the previous stanza is overcome by the child's verbal grenade thrown into the social pond that is 'The Lounge'. The child is 'thrilled' by the powerful effect her words have, in an act that is clearly premeditated. The 'malicious pause' reminds us of the 'sharp hands poised' of stanza 2. The response of the mother's friends can be tasted as it 'salted' the child's tongue 'like an imminent storm'. The anticipation of a storm is something we register physically as well as mentally. The literal meteorological storm becomes the domestic storm that is the 'uproar' of the women's shocked reaction. The mother's reaction is, ironically, to utter another litany, this time a list of her friends' names. Just as language was sanitised by the women's spelling out of words, she reinforces the idea by insisting that her daughter washes dirty words from her mouth with soap.

The last three sentences of the poem modulate into the present tense, introducing a distance between the experience described in the past and the adult poet-self. This self is able to grapple with experience through the very medium that terrified the women the poem presents. At the time of the incident, the child was expected to sit and listen. She learnt a 'code' at her 'mother's knee', pretending not to listen to 'embarrassing' words. The poet's mission now is to *decode* experience through language.

NOSTALGIA

- A group of mercenaries move from a high mountainous settlement to a valley area, motivated by money to join an army outside their own community.
- The emotional and physical effects of their movement are explored.

This poem is, in large measure, an exploration of the history of the word that forms its title, and as such may be viewed as an **etymological** excursion. Nostalgia is generally a desire to return home or a feeling of loss involving longing for the past. In so far as we use the word to mean this it does signify such longing, but the poet is subtly reminding us that we may not always make the right connections or draw the right conclusions from what we genuinely think are empirically observable data. Sometimes our physical, intellectual and emotional responses to situations can become blurred or unreliable.

QUESTION

'Nostalgia' explores the pain of return in more than one sense. Consider other poems of Duffy's that dwell on painful memories, the effects of 'mean time'.

In fact, people who lived at high altitudes in mountainous regions for most of the year, experiencing a pain in the heart on descending to the foothills where the air was less thin, mistakenly thought they were feeling ill as a result of being away from familiar surroundings. Since their hearts ached they assumed an emotional connection with the physical effects accompanying a change of scene. The word nostalgia is derived from the Greek words *nostos* meaning 'return' and *algos* meaning 'pain'. It is therefore reasonable to interpret the term as referring to pain resulting from the desire to return home, but we should not confuse the emotional and physical sources of such pain.

COMMENTARY

Carol Ann Duffy gives voice to the feelings of the people she presents in the poem. Their sense of being placed in unfamiliar, almost foreign surroundings is reflected in the repetition of 'wrong' in the first stanza. Food is 'the wrong taste'; the sounds heard in the thicker air are 'wrong', there are 'wrong smells' and even the 'light' is 'wrong'. Finally, 'every breath' is 'wrong'. This reaction indicates the manner in which a violent physical response to the pain of moving to lower ground, 'It was killing them', swamps judgement. The second stanza begins with the naming of the pain as nostalgia. This results in the mythologising of the word itself as a signifier of the phenomenon of pining for home. The images of homesickness are presented in the emotional appeal of 'sweet pain in the heart', 'music of home', and 'sad pipes – summoning'.

The use of the phrase 'the word was out' at the start of the third stanza reminds us that once an idea becomes fixed in people's minds it is impossible to go back, to put the genie back in the bottle as it were. In Saussurean linguistic terms, once the relationship between signifier and **signified** has been established it is one that remains constant (see **Critical History: The literature act – ways of reading**). Equally, if something is not actually given a name it cannot be experienced. This idea is encapsulated in the third stanza, 'Some would never / fall in love had they not heard of love'. It emphasises that the meaning of words is very much a matter of social agreement, but there needs to be a speech community in the first place if language is to be a living, dynamic system of signification.

Since the poem explores the idea of hankering for the past, it is not inappropriate that its verbs are exclusively in the past tense. The final stanza reflects on some of the consequences of the word nostalgia being 'out'. Two figures of authority – a priest 'crying at the workings of memory' and a schoolteacher smelling the 'scent of her youth, too late' in an opened book – are seen to be suffering emotional trauma resulting from a desire to go back to the time of their youth. One of the 'mercenaries' referred to in the first stanza 'returned' (a reminder of the etymology of 'nostalgia') 'with his life

CHECK THE BOOK
Course in General Linguistics by Ferdinand de Saussure, translated by Roy Harris (1995), is a fine introduction to this important linguist's work.

/ in a sack on his back'. The use of **internal rhyme** emphasises the wistful search for the past. The repetition of the word 'same' like that of 'wrong' in stanza 1 is integral to Duffy's design. The **ironic** tension between the hopeful springtime return of the man and the fact that what was once familiar has now 'changed' forcefully reminds us that we cannot repeat the past, however hard we might try. There may be 'the same sign on the inn' but time has passed, as signalled by the 'chiming' of the 'same bell' – nothing escapes the passage of time.

BEFORE YOU WERE MINE

- Speaking in the voice of her pre-existent self, the poet addresses her mother during the ten-year period preceding her (the poet's) birth.

In this poem Carol Ann Duffy addresses her mother, framing the time element in a curious way so that she inhabits with her voice the ten-year period before she was born. She is exploring real time but a time that can only be imagined as far as she is concerned. Through specific detail she reconstructs the life her mother led before her daughter's birth.

COMMENTARY

The title of the poem is surprising in that it suggests something a mother might say to a child rather than the other way around. The word 'mine' suggests closeness in a relationship and a sense of loving ownership.

CONTEXT

In the 1950s, dance halls and cinemas were the principal places for men and women to meet.

Stanza 1 sees the poet employing the first person in order to address her mother, who is carefree and happy. There is an almost ghostly effect created by the child speaking to the parent before it is born. The sentence 'I'm not here yet', which opens the second stanza, is characteristic of Duffy's treatment of time and creates tension between the present and an anticipated future. These ideas are, of course, projected imaginatively into the past of the poet's mother.

The seemingly arbitrary sequence of events that leads to the existence of us all is somehow short-circuited and lent a kind of inevitability by the background presence of the poet. This is clearly perceptible even though the 'thought' of a daughter does not enter her head while she dances in 'the ballroom with the thousand eyes', a reference to the presence of five hundred potential husbands watching her (line 7). The hoped-for future of the mother is framed in terms of 'fizzy, movie tomorrows / the right walk home could bring'. The word 'fizzy' suggests zest for life and excitement (compare this with 'fizzing hope' in 'The Captain of the 1964 *Top of the Form* Team') as much as capturing the rather hissy soundtracks and the some-times less than sharp picture quality of early films. The 'movie tomorrows' indicate the way young women hoped that their lives would become real-life versions of the films they flocked to see.

The third stanza intensifies the sense of the mother's freedom as her child to be reminds her that she arrived, like all babies, with a 'loud, possessive yell' (line 11). The easy, conversational **tone** of the sentence finishing with 'eh?' underlines the intimacy of a relationship that has been developing for a long time. Duffy turns her attention to the memory of being a little girl doing such things as putting her hands in her mother's 'high-heeled red shoes'. Such an action is fairly typical of what a little girl might do and enables the reader to identify easily with the situation described. The shoes are 'relics', a word that emphasises the gulf of time between the event remembered and the occasion of its recall; it also has a religious **connotation**, implying that the shoes are very special because of their association with the poet's mother. The stanza closes with the poet vividly imagining her youthful mother as she revisits her old Glasgow haunt: 'and now your ghost clatters toward me over George Square / till I see you, clear as scent'. By employing the technique of synaesthesia, Duffy replicates for the reader the vividness of her seemingly visionary experience of her mother. Scent is unmistakable and almost always associated in our minds with a person and a place. As well as sight, the poet is relying on smell, the most evocative of our senses.

The final stanza continues to catalogue the details of childhood memory, the poet fondly recalling the learning of dance steps 'on

CONTEXT

Synaesthesia is the description of a sense impression in terms more appropriate to a different sense – the mixing of sense impressions. The phrase 'I see you, clear as scent' is an example of the technique.

CONTEXT

The 'polka-dot dress' mentioned in the first stanza recalls two famous photographs, one of Monroe strategically stepping over a hot air vent which caused her dress to fly up, and another called 'Seaside Chat', by the photographer Bert Hardy. The women in the latter wear dresses similar to Monroe's, while the photograph is clearly influenced by the image of her.

the way home from Mass'. The **image** of 'stamping stars from the wrong pavement' conjures pictures of Hollywood but reminds us that there is no escaping real life. 'Even then' suggests that the child yearned for her mother even before she was born. This is a tremendously confirmatory idea and it is clear that 'love lasts' for the poet and her mother in the real present as well as the imagined past. The final sentence, peppered with words like 'glamorous', 'sparkle', 'waltz' and 'laugh', suggests youth and enjoyment and signals that, unlike many daughters, the poet can imagine a life for her mother without the children she was later to bear. The final phrase of the poem, which contains a repetition of its title, reminds us of its **ambiguity**. Duffy evokes the Glasgow of the 1950s with its dance halls and fashions influenced by American icons like Marilyn Monroe. The image Duffy creates of her mother with her friends is an idealised, imaginary one – even the names are invented. This is wholly in keeping with the way children try to reconstruct their parents' lives through images already available. Such images often do include photographs.

The poet imagines her mother risking 'a hiding' from her mother (the poet's grandmother) for arriving home late from a dance. This indicates clearly that the relationship between parents and children does not differ significantly from one generation to the next.

VALENTINE

- The persona of the poem presents a lover with an unconventional valentine, confronting them with some discomfiting truths about love and relationships.

This poem subverts or challenges the accepted view of a valentine. The **metaphorical** presentation of an onion as 'a moon wrapped in brown paper' alerts us to the similarity between this poem and those of the **metaphysical poets**, who favoured the **conceit** as a writing technique. The symbolic aspect of the onion is reminiscent of the manner in which they approached ordinary objects in surprising and original ways.

COMMENTARY

Lines 1 and 12 – 'Not a red rose or a satin heart' and 'Not a cute card or a kissogram' – signal immediately that the traditional view of 14 February is being challenged. The actual presentation of a gift is not avoided, though, and is even stressed beyond the first proffering of 'I give you an onion' in the repetition of this sentence in line 13. 'Here' (line 6) and 'Take it' (line 18) further emphasise the insistence of the giver.

Just as the papery outer layers of an onion can be peeled to reveal its fleshy layers, so too can a lover undress to reveal flesh. Also, the **persona** in the poem strips away any layers of falsehood, making the implications of taking on a relationship quite clear. Although the onion may be equated with pleasurable experiences 'like the careful undressing of love', it may just as easily 'blind you with tears / like a lover'. These **similes** point towards the basic truth that human relationships are complex and, like an onion, multilayered. People can be passionate, 'truthful', 'possessive' or 'faithful'. All of these attributes may be found in one individual and each of them may be in conflict with the other person in the relationship at any given time. It is not surprising, therefore, that a lover can 'blind you with tears'. The **image** presented in lines 9–10 conveys the effects of peeling onions with which we are all familiar but also makes the imaginative leap necessary to connect it with the emotional power wielded by a lover.

The second proffering of the onion in line 13 is followed by a truthful statement concerning the implications of accepting it, as was the case in lines 2–5. This time 'careful undressing' is replaced by 'Its fierce kiss will stay on your lips, / possessive and faithful / as we are, / for as long as we are'. This introduces a far more conditional and uncertain dimension as the reader is left wondering just how long the taste of an onion lasts. There are no guarantees being offered here, only risk.

QUESTION

In 'Valentine', Duffy describes love as being 'Lethal'. Consider other poems in *Mean Time* that present the painful and dangerous side of relationships.

Duffy concludes by addressing further the harsh realities of relationships and equates married life with death. The fact that the onion could 'shrink to a wedding ring' clearly indicates that there is a diminution involved in matrimony. The 'platinum loops' recall the earlier reference to the moon and its traditional colour association and also remind us of the precious metal sometimes used to make wedding rings. A loop could be a challenge to the idea as a positive **symbol** of eternity. In a bad relationship the ring will come to symbolise perpetual entrapment. The adjective 'Lethal' reinforces the notion that a long-term relationship is effectively the death of individuality. The implications of committing oneself to a relationship can have lasting import and may 'cling' like the smell of an onion. This idea is further personalised in that there is an implied reference to the scent of a lover's body, which could 'cling to your fingers'. The final line with its uncompromising and potentially violent reference to a knife is in keeping with the preceding honest examination of a relationship. It slices through the onion just as language can be used incisively to reveal the truth.

HAVISHAM

- Miss Havisham, the woman jilted at the altar in Charles Dickens's novel *Great Expectations*, talks of her feelings about her experience.

This **dramatic monologue** is a powerful insight into the potential thoughts and feelings of the character in Charles Dickens's novel *Great Expectations* (1861). Miss Havisham was jilted at the altar and never recovered.

COMMENTARY

A tortured Miss Havisham, riven by the conflict between being in love and hating the man who jilted her, is encapsulated in the first two sentences: 'Beloved sweetheart bastard. Not a day since then / I haven't wished him dead.' The plosive 'b' and dental 'd' sounds immediately establish the bitterness and violent aggression in the

Robert Browning's *Dramatis Personae* was published in 1864. Among the most famous poems in this volume is 'My Last Duchess'. Duffy is well known for her extensive use of the dramatic monologue, something that became the mainstay of her next collection, *The World's Wife*.

woman's voice. The psychological damage done to Miss Havisham is presented in the physical **image** of eyes that have become 'dark green pebbles' and the tendons of her hands are 'ropes' she 'could strangle with'.

The root of her hatred lies in the fact that she is a 'Spinster' (line 5). The word, as a sentence in its own right, is isolated like the woman who is defined by society in terms of her unmarried state. She is so obsessed with her predicament that she spends entire days 'cawing Nooooo at the wall'. The sound suggested is, perhaps, that of a parrot endlessly repeating the same sound. It certainly conveys a visceral, animal-like howling too. Miss Havisham still wears her wedding dress, playing the role of bride, causing her to 'stink and remember'. The sight of the yellowing dress is seen in a 'slewed mirror'. What does this suggest? Seeing herself in the mirror rekindles her hatred of the man who deserted her, resulting in the 'Puce curses' of line 9.

She has dreams that are sexual fantasies about what she might have experienced with the husband she never had. Her 'fluent tongue' explores his body but as she moves near his loins 'I suddenly bite awake'. This suggests that in doing so she could emasculate him with her teeth, re-establishing the overriding emotion of anger that she still feels. The **enjambment** that links stanzas 3 and 4 draws attention to this conflict as it reminds us that such an opposition can coexist in one person. Typographically, the physical distance between the stanzas neatly presents the simultaneous tendency of Miss Havisham to love and hate the man. The mixture of emotions she articulates in line 1 is developed in the **oxymoron** 'Love's / hate behind a white veil' (lines 12–13). This veil, like Havisham, has decayed; it has yellowed and she is physically and mentally diminished. The power of 'red balloon bursting / in my face. Bang' is conveyed again through the use of plosives. Also, through the **onomatopoeic** 'Bang' we see her faced with the truth of her situation erupting through the 'veil' of her dream as she becomes fully conscious. There may also be a subconscious reference to the rupturing of the hymen that she has never experienced. She remembers stabbing her wedding cake, which leads to a disturbing articulation of both homicidal and necrophiliac tendencies.

 QUESTION

Havisham's voice seems to break into sobs at the end of the poem. What else might break besides 'the heart'? What else might her use of a knife suggest?

DISGRACE

- This poem catalogues the breakdown of a relationship that had once been very intense and passionate.

Change is the key to the poem, which highlights the negative effect of time on a relationship. The shadows on the wall are grotesque projected images of the people involved. Duffy chooses to focus our attention on these because they are emblematic of the way the relationship has become distorted. In another sense the relationship is a shadow of its former self.

COMMENTARY

There is a sequence of **images** associated with disease and death running through the poem. Rooms incubate 'a thickening cyst of dust' (stanza 1). Duffy also uses terms directly relating to language, often linking this with death. Words become 'Dead flies in a web', emphasising the idea that the relationship is now a snare. There is a perceptive insight into the way that people tend to continue a relationship long past the point when it has really broken down. Repeated references to waking up show that the truth has a habit of confronting us with what we already knew but did not face. We should be alert to the **metaphorical** signification of 'Woke', which suggests realisation of what has irrevocably changed. The dawning of the day brings with it recognition of 'the absence of grace', a definition of 'disgrace'. So, it is a defining moment in more than one sense. 'We had not been home in our hearts for months' again articulates the truth of the situation.

CHECK THE BOOK

For a good, concise study, see *Carol Ann Duffy* by Deryn Rees-Jones (1999).

The domestic setting becomes the focus of anger, frustration and verbal abuse where there had once been harmony and love. The transition from the calligraphic 'italics' (line 6) to 'obscenities' (line 7) again signals the decline that has occurred. The image of the clothes on the floor as being 'like a corpse' shows how the same sight can have very different effects over time. A sight that once brought with it an erotic charge now only suggests the death of a relationship.

Physical, concrete detail is used to explore the way the relationship has effectively died. The 'small deaths of lightbulbs' are 'audible tears', suggesting both the similarity in shape of a lightbulb and a tear, and the idea that they are weeping over their own extinction, as the lover at the end of the poem does over the finished relationship. The night is now a setting for 'the wrong language', the rows accompanied by 'waving and pointing'. This leads to a disturbing dream 'of a naked crawl / from a dead place over the other; both of us' (lines 15–16). The death image in the dream fuses with reality, though, as the speaker wakes.

In the description 'the still life / of a meal, untouched, wine bottle, empty, ashtray, / full' we are aware of the reference to a painting and that this is only a representation of real life. The phrase 'still life' also suggests death in this context. Nicotine and alcohol fuelled the previous night in place of real nourishment. Neither partner could face food because of emotional upset. The **personified** fridge, with its 'cool heart' indifferent to their suffering, 'hummed'. It is described as 'selfish as art', indicating a detachment that is able to represent even a trauma such as this. It is certainly legitimate to observe that this is precisely what 'Disgrace' does.

The penultimate stanza presents the eruption of the anger and frustration of the lovers through the effect they have on what was once their shared home: the alarm is 'screaming', the door 'banging' and the house plants 'trembling'.

The conclusion of the poem conveys hopelessness, intransigence and desolation. One of the former lovers counts 'the years to arrive there', a highly negative thought. The stars are 'meaningless', perhaps suggesting that they can offer no source of solace. Both people are 'lost' and the 'Inconsolable vowels' of the other partner reiterate the death of meaningful communication. The sound of sobbing is suggested. The phrase 'you / and me both' usually implies closeness but here it is conveying mutual loss or disorientation. Their separateness is emphasised by the line break.

> **? QUESTION**
>
> How does Duffy's choice of a sequence of eight unrhymed **quatrains** suit her subject matter in 'Disgrace'?

> ## MEAN TIME
>
> - This poem gives the collection its title.
> - It explores the destructive effects of time and the breakdown of a relationship.

The speaker in the poem bemoans the end of a relationship and looks back over it, regretting some of the exchanges of its final days. The **imagery** is mournful and its outlook bleak. The style is terse and unadorned.

QUESTION

What is the effectiveness of *Mean Time* as a title for Duffy's fourth collection? Trace the theme of time and its effects through a consideration of the poet's use of imagery.

COMMENTARY

People in Britain are familiar with the changes that occur in both summer and winter when the clocks are altered. Carol Ann Duffy refers to the winter shift when evenings become dark more quickly. In claiming the clocks 'stole light from my life' a real sense of both grievance and grieving is communicated. This is compounded by the emotional turmoil conveyed in the funereal image 'mourning our love' (line 4). The journey away from the lover is made 'through the wrong part of town' and the image of 'unmendable rain' is directly applicable to the fractured relationship. In 'bleak streets' the distraught **persona** sifts through the past. 'I felt my heart gnaw / at all our mistakes' (lines 7–8). Regret over the most recent cruel exchanges is articulated in the third stanza but time has passed, never to be recovered, and the words have been said. In this way the situation is as 'unmendable' as the rain mentioned in stanza 2.

The final stanza confronts the finality of death and ruefully observes that the very mechanism we use to regulate our lives seems, at the time of year presented, to be calculatingly truncating them, resulting in 'shortened days'. The **hyperbolic** reference to 'endless nights' reflects the sense of all-consuming darkness that is commonly felt during the melancholic aftermath of an important relationship. This pessimistic conclusion is a counterblast to a belief in eternal light and emphasises the idea that our present existence is the only one we have. As a result of this we are led to reflect upon the tyranny of time and the way in which we are in its thrall. The **personification** of the clocks that steal time surreptitiously is effectively conveyed by 'slid' in the opening line.

The brevity of this poem belies the profundity of its concerns. As the penultimate poem in *Mean Time* it revisits the recurrent themes of love, life, loss, death and time that have been explored throughout the collection. Its distillation of these concerns to what seems to be an unremittingly pessimistic view of life and absence of consolation is, however, mitigated by the next poem, 'Prayer'.

PRAYER

- In the absence of a conventionally religious faith, the poet seeks solace in a secular version of prayer.

This is a **sonnet**, an appropriate choice of form for concentrated thought or contemplation. Although this is very much a secular or non-religious poem, it clearly elevates ordinary experience and memories and lends them great significance. A prayer is normally associated with the liturgical, but this sonnet offers a framework for the non-religious. In much the same way as William Wordsworth did, Carol Ann Duffy finds 'solace in the sonnet's scanty plot of ground'. 'Prayer' also seems rooted in Wordsworth's dictum that poetry should be something that 'cherishes our daily lives'. In following the rhyme scheme of a Shakespearean sonnet, modern concerns find a traditional form of containment.

CHECK THE BOOK
Don Paterson's *101 Sonnets: From Shakespeare to Heaney* (1999) offers an excellent introduction to the form and a fine selection of poems. A more comprehensive treatment is given in *The Penguin Book of the Sonnet: 500 Years of a Classic Tradition in English*, edited by Phillis Levin (2001).

The wistful **tone** and measured **cadence** create a contemplative space in what is very often a fraught and frenetic life. Images of a remembered, less complicated, secure childhood effectively transcend an unpalatable present and insecure adult sense of temporariness.

COMMENTARY

The first **quatrain** presents the illuminating 'sudden gift' to a woman who, attracted by what seems to be music, 'will lift /

'PRAYER' continued

CONTEXT

A minim is a musical note with a value of two beats.

CONTEXT

The sonnet first came to prominence in Italy. Francis Petrarch's sonnets to Laura established the form as a medium for the expression of love. Sir Thomas Wyatt and the Earl of Surrey introduced the sonnet to England in the sixteenth century, where it was adapted by Shakespeare and later by John Milton. Other notable sonneteers are John Donne, William Wordsworth, Elizabeth Barrett Browning, Gerard Manley Hopkins, Seamus Heaney and Tony Harrison.

her head from the sieve of her hands and stare / at the minims sung by a tree'. Normally people say prayers but this one mysteriously 'utters itself'. This suggests a welcome release from worry brought about by what James Joyce termed an epiphany. The 'minims sung by a tree' could refer to birds singing in it or it might be a deliberately **surreal image**. Whatever the explanation, it seems that an unbidden blessing has occurred that offers temporary joy for a careworn woman.

The consoling quality of memory is explored in the second quatrain as a man is described listening to a train and identifying the sound it makes with the rhythm of the Latin verbs he declined as a boy. The example 'amabo, amabas, amabant' is enough to illustrate this. It also introduces the idea of repetition as an important factor in prayer. The words themselves become less significant as the mind is able to disengage itself from humdrum concerns as the mantric rhythm persists. The fact that the train is 'distant' refers to the man's aural perception of it but also suggests the gulf of time between his adult and childhood selves.

'Pray for us now' at the opening of the final quatrain is taken from a Catholic prayer to the Virgin Mary with its concluding line: 'Pray for us now and at the hour of our death'. Here, emphasis on the present reinforces the sense of cherishing moments of insight or consolation while we can, rather than dwelling on death. Also, the sentence might be a means of presenting a fragment of a now discarded religious practice that has been assimilated into a new, secular way of praying. The lodger who likes to hear piano scales being practised and the person who 'calls / a child's name as though they named their loss' are both brought into communion with their own childhood just as the man who heard the train was. It is striking that all three people, 'a woman', 'a man' and 'the lodger' are arrested by a sound. This is in keeping with prayer as utterance or performance leading to reflection. This is the process all these people go through.

The concluding **couplet** begins with the contrast of the 'Darkness outside' and the familiarity of a domestic interior. The 'radio's prayer' refers to the shipping forecast, the sprung rhythms of which have entranced many thousands of people, not just poets. Duffy suggests that the sound of the list of place names is like that of a conventional litany. The rhyme of 'radio's prayer' and 'Finisterre' closes the poem in a calm, soothing fashion. The pronunciation of both words involves gentle expiration of air, lending them a whispered quality. Technically this is known as aspiration, which, in another sense, encapsulates what praying is all about. The metrical characteristics of the final line are also worth noting. Whereas the three **quatrains** are basically **iambic**, the couplet employs trochees and **dactyls** to create a falling-off effect at the end of these lines:

> Darkness outside. Inside, the radio's prayer –
> Rockall. Malin. Dogger. Finisterre.

As if this sense of conclusion were not powerful enough, it is important to consider that Finisterre was the word used on ancient maps to indicate land's end, or edge of the earth. So, just as the word implies an absolute limit, this secular prayer is bound very firmly within the confines of a sonnet.

OTHER POEMS

The poems in this section of *New Selected Poems 1984–2004* are not taken from a discrete collection. They were written between the composition of *Mean Time* and *The World's Wife*.

A CHILD'S SLEEP

- The poet reflects on the beauty of childhood innocence as she watches her daughter sleep.

Clearly about the poet's daughter, this tender poem expresses a reverential love and articulates gratitude for the beauty of an innocent sleeping child and the maternal impulse in nature.

 QUESTION

What might 'Darkness outside' (line 13) suggest beyond the obvious?

CONTEXT

A trochee is a metrical foot of two syllables in which the accent or stress falls on the first syllable.

COMMENTARY

Even the potentially frightening aspects of the night are rendered benign by 'The greater dark / outside the room' that is 'maternal, wise, / with its face of moon.' The adult and child are separated by the mystery of sleep. Duffy presents her child's sleep as being charged with the magic of fairy tales. There is something simultaneously accessible and exclusive about the child's innocent sleep that is so different from an adult's: 'although I could not enter there, / I could not leave' (lines 3–4). The child's sleep is presented **metaphorically** as a 'small wood' that is 'dark, peaceful, sacred, / acred in hours' (lines 7–8). The **internal rhyme** that also turns the noun 'acre' into a verb 'acred' neatly links the **images** of a wood and flowers already used and emphasises the way a child's time is so much more expansive than an adult's.

The five open **quatrains** employ rhyme sparingly using an *abcb* scheme. The third stanza is both the thematic and structural pivot of the poem. The sleeping child is the embodiment of goodness that is beyond temporal or linguistic boundaries: 'without time, without history, / wordlessly good' (lines 11–12). The poet's love for her daughter moves her to say her name, which is 'a pebble dropped / in the still night' (lines 13–14), and results in the child stirring because, even in sleep, she registers her mother's voice. The pebble image suggests ripples moving outwards from the centre as well as a noise that interrupts the silence. The significance of the child as the centre of the parent's life is clear. Her 'palms / cupping their soft light' (lines 15–16) sustain the mood of calm Duffy creates throughout the poem.

CONTEXT

Twenty-three of the forty-three people on board the aeroplane died. Eight members of Sir Matt Busby's team were killed. The most famous survivor of the Munich air crash is Sir Bobby Charlton.

MUNICH

- The deaths of the 'Busby Babes', the young Manchester United footballers, are commemorated.

This short poem takes images associated with football and uses them in ways that we do not expect so as to draw attention to the tragedy of 6 February 1958.

COMMENTARY

The blizzard that led to the crash is likened to a 'frenzied crowd', but the desolation of the outcome is captured in 'Nobody cheered or booed' (line 2). This also points to the fact that anyone hearing the terrible news of the players' deaths was shocked; the event obliterated any partisan response from anyone who might support a team other than Manchester United. The aeroplane is presented as if it were a footballer as it takes 'Two runs at take-off' (line 3).

The extended **metaphor** continues with the plummeting of the plane to earth described as 'a full-time blow on the whistle' (line 7). The full stop at the end of the line emphasises the finality of death. The final stanza takes a football manager's **cliché** – 'Not over the moon' – and turns it into a negative, sober truth. The list of the names of those who died is 'pinned up like a hand-picked team'. Normally, any footballer is considered lucky if chosen to play for the most famous team in the world, but there is a clear sense that these men were chosen by the hand of fate.

TO BOIL BACON

- A married woman prepares a bacon joint and hears a news report on the radio telling of the abdication of King Edward VIII.

Edward VIII abdicated on 11 December 1936 after the prime minster, Stanley Baldwin, told him that the British people would not accept Wallis Simpson, an American divorcee, as the British queen. His abdication speech was broadcast on the radio.

CHECK THE NET
Search the Internet for an abdication timeline of Edward VIII.

COMMENTARY

The poem is written in the form of a recipe describing the process of preparing and cooking a bacon joint, but in a way that provides a commentary on the domestic situation of the woman, who seems trapped in her marriage and certainly will not be able to escape

her situation as the king managed to do. Britain was in the grip
of a terrible economic recession and boiled bacon was a staple
food for poor people. The lot of working people had not really
improved since the General Strike of 1926. Women had only been
given the vote in 1928 and, with the rise of Fascism, Europe was
teetering on the brink of a second world war. These details are
not dealt with directly in the poem, but the reference to one of
the most famous broadcasts in history can do nothing but call
them to mind as the reader is faced with the contrast between the
ordinary woman in straitened circumstances and the relationship
between a king and a commoner. We are invited to consider the
hardship faced by the woman boiling bacon. She has no choice,
even if it is a tough decision to give up a position as powerful
as the monarchy.

TO THE UNKNOWN LOVER

- Any potential lover is warned off by the persona in the
  poem in order that the inevitable ensuing pain involved
  may be avoided.

QUESTION

How does Duffy
use aspects of
popular culture
in this poem?

The voice articulated in this poem is one that speaks with experience
learnt the emotional hard way, and one that is suspicious of anyone
who might lead to romantic involvement.

COMMENTARY

The opening stanza is a powerful statement about the pain a lover
can inflict and is therefore 'Horrifying' to imagine, the potential
lover being a 'knife' that can wound, leaving a permanent scar.
This **image** reminds us that past relationships, though invisible
on the outside, can leave permanent psychological scars. By using
fragments of popular songs that sentimentalise romantic love, and
things associated with the beginnings of relationships such as going
out for dinner and telephone calls, the full impact of the risks we
take when making an emotional commitment to someone else is
brought into sharp focus. The first line of stanza 3 – 'This old heart

of mine's' – is the opening of a song that continues with the words 'been broke a thousand times', but Duffy chooses to use the image of 'an empty purse' to indicate that being spent up is the result of damaging relationships. In contrast, the **persona** in the original song tries yet again with a new lover. The last two stanzas key into popular culture by inverting first a famous song, and then the immortal line 'Here's looking at you, kid' from the film *Casablanca*. The song 'As Time Goes By' begins: 'You must remember this / A kiss is still a kiss'. At one point in *Casablanca*, Ilsa says to Rick, 'Kiss me. Kiss me as if it were the last time.' The intensity of their relationship at this point in the film is later matched by the pain of their ultimate parting. The final, emphatic one-line stanza of the poem – 'Here's not looking, kid, at you' – is used by Duffy to draw attention to the fact that bitter experience teaches us self-preservation and the ability to make our heads rule our hearts. However 'handsome, beautiful, drop-dead / gorgeous' (stanza 2) any unknown lover may be, they are just not worth the risk of knowing in case they cause unbearable pain. Despite the emphatic reversal of Rick's famous line, we cannot help but observe that for every person who manages to learn from past experiences, there will be many more who become involved in a new relationship only to be hurt again.

THE WORLD'S WIFE

All the poems in *The World's Wife* are **dramatic monologues**, with the exception of 'The Kray Sisters', which is written in the composite voice of two women. Carol Ann Duffy invents none of the stories that form the basis of the poems. She has taken some well-known characters from **myth** and history, exploring aspects of their lives and personalities in ways that interrogate them in fresh, humorous and thought-provoking ways. The title of the collection clearly signals that the poems will be written from a female perspective, one that takes the saying 'the world and his wife' and reminds us that the world is not owned by men as the possessive pronoun 'his' suggests. The opening lines of 'Mrs Beast' read rather like a manifesto for the collection as a whole:

CHECK THE FILM
The 1942 film *Casablanca* starred Humphrey Bogart as Rick Blaine and Ingrid Bergman as Ilsa Lund.

CHECK THE BOOK
Jeffrey Wainwright's essay 'Female metamorphoses: Carol Ann Duffy's Ovid' is a fine discussion of *The World's Wife* in *The Poetry of Carol Ann Duffy: 'Choosing Tough Words'*, edited by Angelica Michelis and Antony Rowland, pp. 47–55 (2003).

These myths going round, these legends, fairy tales,
I'll put them straight; so when you stare
into my face – Helen's face, Cleopatra's,
Queen of Sheba's, Juliet's – then, deeper,
gaze into my eyes – Nefertiti's, Mona Lisa's,
Garbo's eyes – think again.

The women mentioned were all pursued by men or are regarded
as icons of desire. Some of the men who fell in love with them were
very powerful or handsome. Mrs Beast speaks for all women and is
advocating a beast as a partner rather than a prince because 'The sex
/ is better.' She toasts Fay Wray, the woman who enchanted King
Kong, and in unsentimental vein closes the poem with the words
'Let the less-loving one be me.' This challenges **stereotypical** views
about women's behaviour and places them in a position of power
over men.

CONTEXT

The language used
in *The World's
Wife* ranges from
the cockney
rhyming **argot**
of the Kray sisters
to the lyricism of
Anne Hathaway.

Through making individual women's voices heard, the poet builds
up what amounts to an orchestra of individual women's voices
resulting in a collective female chorus. These voices are often either
forgotten or disregarded in a world that lionises men but often
marginalises the women who live with them, are wives or lovers to
them. Above all, the female voices emerge as intellectually capable
and aware of their own potentials. Such potential can be wasted and
this stifling is very much a tragedy in the strict sense that sacrifice
is involved. The fatal flaw in men, their hubris, is presented as
something that affects women and not just themselves.

The predicament of women is not presented simply in terms of
shoddy treatment at the hands of men. Carol Ann Duffy's feminism
is not of the type that derides men for being men. She makes it clear
that being an **apologist** for such attitudes reduces the argument to
the level of those blinkered men who might dismiss women as being
less worthy of attention than they are simply by virtue of their
gender. This is not to say, of course, that men escape criticism.

MRS MIDAS

- King Midas, having been granted a wish, decided that he would like all that he touched to turn to gold.
- The poem explores the consequences of this from the point of view of his long-suffering wife.

Duffy presents a wide range of emotions through the **persona** of Mrs Midas. She is exasperated by her husband's selfishness and resents the curtailment of sexual relations with him. He is a 'fool' who could not think beyond his own short-term greed. In her railing against him there is also a good deal that is humorous. This humour arises partly out of the powerfully imagined life that Duffy outlines, and partly from universally identifiable weaknesses that Mrs Midas complains about in her husband.

COMMENTARY

The opening of the poem creates a mood of nonchalant domesticity and this accentuates the contrasting bizarre events that follow. Mrs Midas had 'begun / to unwind' and the **personified** kitchen 'filled with the smell of itself, relaxed, its steamy breath / gently blanching the windows'. The word 'blanching', itself a cooking term, helps to establish what is being done. The open window provides ventilation and the other is wiped to reveal the murky evening, leading Mrs Midas to doubt, at first, what she sees. Duffy introduces details such as the **image** of the pear turning into what looks 'like a lightbulb. On.' The comic effect is intensified through the use of the full stop followed by a single word sentence at the end of line 11. Mrs Midas's speculation about fairy lights is also whimsical and acts as a direct contrast to what turns out to be a very serious matter.

The third stanza's description of Midas transforming the kitchen, particularly its blinds, into gold, provokes his wife to remember her history lessons at school with Miss Macready, who taught her about the Field of the Cloth of Gold. Midas's chair becomes a 'burnished throne' and his 'strange, wild, vain' look signals that he realises that he has been given the tremendous power he asked for, about which,

CONTEXT

The Field of the Cloth of Gold was the meeting place between Guînes and Ardres near Calais in France, where Henry VIII of England and Francis I of France and their entourages gathered between 7 and 24 June 1520. The castles at both villages were in a state of decay, and therefore splendid temporary palaces and pavilions were erected for Henry at Guînes and for Francis at Ardres.

at this point, his wife knows nothing. Naturally, she asks, 'What in the name of God is going on?' This emphatic interrogative sentence is a deftly accurate presentation of an exasperated wife faced with the latest example of an infuriating husband's behaviour.

The comic **tone** is maintained and developed as the transformation of everyday food items and domestic implements is catalogued in stanza 4. The sight of these changes causes Mrs Midas to panic as she realises that she could be turned to gold next. In particular, the observed physical process of a wine glass turning to gold conveys her thought process. We sense her reaching a terrible conclusion and the line 'glass, goblet, golden chalice' neatly conveys through **alliteration** of hard 'g' sounds the concrete reality of what is happening, as well as linking the three nouns as names for alternative drinking vessels. The 'l' sounds emphasise increasing luxury culminating in the vowel/consonant blend of 'o' and 'l' in 'golden' which highlights Midas's savouring of the experience with his lips and tongue, and the malleable softness of pure gold.

CHECK THE NET

For information about the fact and fiction of King Midas, search **http://www. phrygians.com**

The remainder of the poem concentrates on the implications of Midas's gift. Mrs Midas continues her account of their relationship in a way that shows she maintains a sense of humour, despite the terrible consequences of what is happening. 'At least, / I said, you'll be able to give up smoking for good' (lines 35–6) and 'He was below, turning the spare room / into the tomb of Tutankhamun' (lines 38–9) are just two examples of this.

The familiar moral of the Midas **myth** is not neglected, though, as Mrs Midas muses on the emptiness of seeking wealth for its own sake. While acknowledging that everyone has dreams: 'Look, we all have wishes; granted' (line 31), she ruefully observes that Midas 'has wishes granted'. The humorous use of 'granted' in two senses leads to the observation that gold 'feeds no one' and 'slakes / no thirst'.

The damage done to their relationship is summarised in 'Separate beds', while Mrs Midas protecting herself from being turned into gold is 'near petrified' as she fears her husband's touch. This is a poignant detail since to be 'petrified' is to be turned to stone. Harsh reality is again emphasised. The physical deprivation suffered by

Mrs Midas is conveyed through the details of a passionate relationship in which the lovers are described 'unwrapping each other, rapidly, / like presents, fast food' (lines 40–1). Midas's 'honeyed embrace' would usually be associated with sweetness but it is its colour similarity with gold that is focused on here.

The dream of a child Mrs Midas has is very poignant, as she will never be able to have a real baby. The popular **metaphor** 'a heart of gold' to describe a person who cares for others is **ironically** inverted as the literal reality of such a phenomenon is presented. The 'ore limbs' and tongue 'like a precious latch' are superficially attractive but 'its amber eyes / holding their pupils like flies' introduces a solid, lifeless element that is ultimately disturbing. Sadly, Mrs Midas can only produce 'dream milk'; 'streaming sun' wakens her, a reminder of gold and of the fact that she will never stream with milk. The **internal rhymes** of 'eyes / flies' and 'dream / streaming' intensify the interior, personal aspect of this woman's experience and the fact that she will have a solitary life foisted on her.

The final sentence reminds us of the popular knowledge of the Midas touch and the physical deprivation of his wife. We are left with the impression that, in spite of feeling aggrieved, there is still a sense of wistfulness associated with desire for her husband and the days when physical relations were possible. As she says, it was 'Pure selfishness' that led him to make the wish with no thought for her or the consequences. Here, Duffy is reminding the reader that the story of Midas is normally viewed purely in connection with the effect his actions had on him, and not on his wife who can only 'dream' of having a child.

> **CONTEXT**
> Pan (stanza 10) was the Greek god of shepherds and flocks.

FROM MRS TIRESIAS

- Mrs Tiresias tells the story of how her husband was transformed into a woman and the effect this had on their relationship.

There are elements of this poem akin to those in 'Mrs Midas'. Both women have husbands who are changed radically in some way, but the consequences of such a change are different in that Mrs Tiresias moves on to a new life with a female lover and does not end up isolated like Mrs Midas. There is a humorous element in this poem too, but the target of all the jokes is Tiresias, who is portrayed as a tedious man and a self-pitying woman.

COMMENTARY

The ordinary language of Mrs Tiresias with her references to 'gardening kecks' and 'Harris tweed' paints a picture of a country couple close to the land. It is clear that Mrs Tiresias is more observant, as she notices the first cuckoo of spring but humours her husband by letting him believe that he does. The innocuous details of the cuckoo in stanza 4 are replaced by the 'faint sneer of thunder' in stanza 5 that causes Mrs Tiresias to feel 'a sudden heat'. The impending storm presages calamity in her life. This is confirmed as she sees the reflection of her transformed husband in the mirror.

Mrs Tiresias's practicality and forbearance are emphasised in the way she helps her husband to deal with the new experience of being a woman. Duffy's choice of details is very funny and the image of a man/woman being taught to blow-dry his hair and borrowing his wife's clothes can only amuse. However, the self-pitying, insufferable aspect of the man does not seem to be something he has shaken off with his transformation, as evidenced by his response to his period starting. The fact that Duffy chooses to write 'Then he started his period' shows that she wishes to show that if men had to suffer '*the curse*' (line 54) they would not face it with such fortitude as women. The ludicrous overreaction of Tiresias – 'One week in bed. / Two doctors in. / Three painkillers four times a day' – makes the point forcibly. Just as Mrs Midas reached a point where she could no longer bear to live with her husband, so does Mrs Tiresias. The last straw is her husband's refusal to be physically close to her for fear of them being taken for lesbians. As he/she says, '*I don't want folk getting the wrong idea*' (line 57). This does not stop him having relationships with 'powerful men', so it comes as little surprise that Mrs Tiresias, having put up with his 'flirt's smile' and refusal to have sex, should

CONTEXT

Kecks is a term for trousers or pants, commonly used in Liverpool. Harris tweed is a famous Scottish brand of cloth used for making jackets.

CONTEXT

While walking on Mount Cyllene, Tiresias saw two snakes mating and, depending upon which version of the story is accepted, separated them, wounded them or killed the female. As a result of this he was transformed into a woman, but regained his male sex by intervening in the same way when he again discovered, in the same spot, the pair of snakes mating. Another version has Tiresias alternating between being a man and a woman every seven years.

take refuge in a lesbian relationship herself. It is **ironic** that in separating a pair of coupling heterosexual snakes, Tiresias was symbolically killing the relationship between himself and his wife. He is to contemplate the 'red wet cry in the night' of his wife with her lover. She savours him imagining 'her bite at the fruit of my lips' (line 87). This is suggestive of the lips of her mouth and of her genitals. Both confusion and clarity are conveyed in 'I noticed then his hands, her hands' (line 92), as the pronouns 'his' and 'her' can apply to two different people or to the dual gender of Tiresias. This works so effectively because Duffy uses the comma **ambiguously** either to indicate apposition or the listing of genitives. The final **image** of 'the clash of their sparkling rings and their painted nails' neatly encapsulates the complexity of gender roles and changes explored in the poem. The conflict is not simply between Tiresias and his wife's lover but within himself as a bifurcated being.

In the Greek **myth**, Tiresias was consulted by Hera, who had been arguing with Zeus about whether the man or the woman experienced the greater pleasure during lovemaking. Tiresias reported that the woman derives nine parts of the pleasure and the man one. The relevance of this is the manner in which sexual experience becomes a central theme. Such experience is not static and certainly not confined to Tiresias, whose wife discovers gratification with another woman. Applying Tiresias's original measure of pleasure it would appear that he and his 'powerful men' enjoy eight tenths less in combination than two women do. Irony is clearly directed against men through one who 'as a woman himself' knows how women feel.

The title '*from* Mrs Tiresias' is a joke in that Carol Ann Duffy is suggesting that the poem is from a larger, more learned work. Having read the poem in public on one occasion, an academic pointed out that some of the story was missing. She was, naturally, concentrating on those elements that suited her purpose in the poem and is thus **satirising** those who over-intellectualise.

> **CONTEXT**
>
> In Sophocles' play *Oedipus Rex*, Tiresias is a blind seer. Duffy focuses on Ovid's *Metamorphoses*.

MRS AESOP

- As the woman on the receiving end of all Aesop's fables in the making, his wife takes revenge by questioning his manhood.

The long-suffering wife of the man who became a household name through his proverbial tales is given the chance in this **dramatic monologue** to tell a story of her own.

COMMENTARY

Aesop could, she says, 'bore for Purgatory', indicating the pain involved in enduring his stories. She presents him as a man of small physical stature (this is factually accurate) who feels the need to compensate for this by building an edifice of proverbial wisdom around himself in the form of countless fables. She is dismissive of his stories, as she knows the real circumstances surrounding them. For example, she reductively and humorously recounts that the 'bird in his hand shat on his sleeve' (line 4). The one-word sentence at the end of the first stanza summarises Mrs Aesop's attitude to her husband: 'Tedious.' She is vindicated in this response as the reader is apprised of his behaviour when walking with his wife. In a humorous, imaginative recreation of what it must have been like to go out with a man like Aesop, Carol Ann Duffy has her reporting the tedium of enduring his searches for 'a shy mouse' or 'a sly fox', suggesting that his fables owed more to confection than observation. He cannot even pass through his garden gate without considering the consequences: 'He'd stand at our gate, look, then leap' (line 6).

The famous fable of the tortoise and the hare is viewed from a new perspective as Mrs Aesop observes that the former was 'creeping, slow as marriage, up the road'. The unremitting tedium is obvious, as is her contempt for him in another one-word dismissal: 'Asshole' (line 15).

Having catalogued the seemingly endless stream of platitudinous moralising from her husband featuring 'sour grapes', a 'sow's ear', and so on, she finally loses patience when he tells her, '*Action, Mrs A., speaks louder / than words*' (lines 19–20). This prompts her to observe that 'the sex / was diabolical'. In an act of revenge she tells her husband her own fable based on a 'little cock that wouldn't crow' (line 22). The word 'cock' is **slang** for penis and it is unable to become erect, as 'wouldn't crow' indicates. In addition to the berating of her husband for his sexual dysfunction, she threatens, '*I'll cut off your tail, all right*'. She concludes by arrogating to herself, in a way that transfers the balance of power from the male to the female, the famous phrase 'He who laughs last laughs longest' in saying, 'I laughed last, longest.'

The infamous case of Loretta Bobbit whose name gave the English language the verb 'to bobbit' is a spectre looming over the male ego and is clearly **alluded** to in this poem. She cut off her husband's penis with a knife and threw it out of a car window. Police later discovered it on a kerbside. This, along with the example of another woman who severed her husband's penis before attaching it to a hot-air balloon and sending it skywards, emphasises the extreme lengths to which some women will go in order to assert themselves, or to which they are pushed by their partners. While the Bobbit case involved a physical emasculation, Mrs Aesop is able to effect a linguistic equivalent which, it might be argued, is more damaging since it is part of a larger discourse that questions male potency in its widest sense.

CHECK THE NET

Go to **http://www.aesopfables.com** if you would like to read any of Aesop's fables.

MRS FAUST

- The wife of the man who famously sold his soul in a pact with the devil tells the story of their life together.
- She reveals that he never had a soul to sell in the first place.

Carol Ann Duffy chooses to place Faust and his wife in the context of a late twentieth-century western consumer environment, one most suitable for the exploration of the materialist and temporal impulse that informs the characters in question.

CONTEXT

In Catholic theology purgatory is a place of atonement between heaven and hell where penitent sinners are required to spend time being purged or cleansed by fire before being deemed fit for heaven.

COMMENTARY

Although attracted to the acquisitive lifestyle and benefits of wealth, Mrs Faust craves something beyond the superficial. Her husband's use of 'whores' drives her to seek solace in such things as 'yoga, t'ai chi, / feng shui', but these offer little relief for a woman who has to face the increasingly frequent and extravagant infidelities of a husband whose libido seems to be directly linked with financial success. He appears to need to celebrate it by taking 'his lust' to prostitutes. As is often the case with men who seem to have everything, Faust 'wanted more'. His lust for power can only be granted to him by someone who is more powerful than he is. The 'oddly sexy' smell of the cigar (a phallic **symbol**) that Mrs Faust detects as her husband strikes his deal with the devil is an acute observation of the link between sex and power. The seemingly endless list of sex scandals associated with powerful men is well known.

Following his pact, the sexual association with power is reinforced in stanza 6: '*the world, / as Faust said, / spread its legs*'. His connection '*with Mephistopheles, / the Devil's boy*' leads to even greater worldly success to the point where he 'knew more than God'. As he goes into what may be literally described as orbit, 'walked on the moon', we realise that Faust, as in the original story, is being used as an emblematic figure whose greed will surely destroy him. His wife's casual unconcern for what he has done is humorously drawn in her observation that 'the clever, cunning, callous bastard / didn't have a soul to sell'. She kept his secret from the devil, suggesting that she is, in some ways, quite proud of his successful deception despite herself. It also demonstrates that, unlike the Faust in Goethe or Marlowe's version, he did not put himself in any metaphysical danger. This is a demonstration by Duffy that in the late twentieth century, with its predilection for the material and rejection of what it sees as medieval beliefs, the power of the **myth** itself is diminished within the terms of its original reference. This does not prevent it, however, from becoming even more resonant as a critique upon a society that has sold everything, including its principles. At least Faust had something with which to pay his debt: he survived on demonic credit but had to settle his account ultimately. Duffy's Faust, on the other hand, knew very well that he could not meet his debt. In this way, the poet is rewriting the fable for a late twentieth-century capitalist society.

The fast life that Faust and his wife lead is characterised by 'Fast cars' and the litany of material possessions catalogued in stanza 2. Although they seem to have earned access to wealth through hard academic study – 'BA. MA. Ph.D.' – they have 'No kids' (line 8). It is success that concerns them rather than education for its own sake.

In the legend, Faust sold his soul to the devil in return for (in most versions) twenty-four years of unlimited power, knowledge and licentiousness. After the allotted period he was dragged down into hell. Here, Mrs Faust reminds us that self-obsessed hedonists are soulless. Faust actually manages to swindle the devil himself in the biggest business deal he has ever pulled off.

CHECK THE BOOK

Doctor Faustus by Christopher Marlowe (published in 1604) is a fascinating play, and the story that underpins Duffy's poem.

QUEEN KONG

- The female equivalent of King Kong talks of her abduction of and infatuation with a natural history film-maker who had visited her island to make a documentary about rare toads.

The reversal of roles in this poem is indicative of the manner in which Carol Ann Duffy draws attention to the fact that the perennial 'Beauty and the Beast' motif can be viewed from the perspective of the female. The enormous power of Queen Kong in relation to the tiny man she falls in love with emphasises the control women can have over men.

COMMENTARY

The opening stanza presents Queen Kong reminiscing about her time in Manhattan after she had decided to pursue her 'little man' (line 2). Duffy humorously has the gorilla reporting that people in 'the Village' (line 5) did not notice her as they 'were used to strangers'. Greenwich Village, a district of New York, is well known

CHECK THE FILM

The original *King Kong* film, in which a giant ape kidnaps Fay Wray, was released in 1933. There was a 1976 remake starring Jeff Bridges and Jessica Lange.

as the dwelling place of bohemian people but to imagine that a gargantuan gorilla could live there without causing a stir is absurd. The added humour of Queen Kong stating that she is 'especially fond of pastrami on rye' as a result of living there conveys a **satirical** view of those who have spent time in New York and claim to have had their lives changed by the experience.

The second stanza makes it clear that the first functions like a flashback in a film as Queen Kong is now speaking from her own home. This technique is appropriate to the fact that *King Kong* was a film and that a film crew arrived 'to make a film' (line 10), a documentary about toads. She goes on to articulate her love for the man in **clichéd** and humorous terms: 'it was absolutely love at first sight' (line 14); 'All right, he was small, but perfectly formed / and *gorgeous*' (lines 17–18). Her physical relationship with the man delights her and this largely has its origins in the difference in size between them. She enjoys the 'things he could do / for me with the sweet finesse of those hands / that no gorilla could' (lines 18–20). This highlights the sexual need he stirs in her but also raises the spectre of bestiality in reverse. She enjoys undressing him: 'I'd gently pick / at his shirt and his trews' (lines 26–7), and like a piece of fruit, possibly a banana, would 'peel him' (line 27). The 'grape of his flesh' (line 28) could refer to his whole body or, perhaps, his glans penis.

The emotional effects of being separated from the man after he leaves are catalogued in stanza 6. She exhibits the characteristic self-neglect associated with someone who feels bereft, as might be reported in a women's magazine: 'I slept for a week, / then woke to binge for a fortnight. I didn't wash' (lines 36–7). The sexual cycle of the female analogous to that of the moon is also emphasised: 'I lasted a month' (line 36); 'I bled when a fat, red moon rolled on the jungle roof' (line 41). After she has decided 'to get him back' the location shifts again to America.

The humorous disjunction between what Queen Kong reports and what is likely to be the case is highlighted in stanza 7, where she says, 'I was discreet, prowled / those streets in darkness'. Even at night a creature of her proportions would surely not escape notice.

Having discovered her man (stanza 8) with a photograph of
her above his bed she celebrates by going on a shopping spree:
'Clothes for my man, mainly, / but one or two treats for myself
from Bloomingdale's'. The comic element remains here as visions of
an impossibly huge primate shopping in exclusive places are created
in the mind of the reader.

The difference in scale between man and creature is further
emphasised in stanza 9: 'I picked him, like a chocolate from the
top layer'. In this **simile** he is presented as something sweet but
also utterly powerless to resist being taken from his room. This
is developed in the way Queen Kong 'let him dangle in the air
between my finger / and my thumb in a teasing, lover's way'.
Again, there is an absurdly comic element introduced as, for the
man, this could be a terrifying experience. Queen Kong's dismissal
of helicopters as 'dragonflies' reinforces her physical size and
power, throwing into even sharper focus the terror of being placed
on 'the tip of the Empire State Building'. It also relates to the point
in stanza 5 when she asks, 'Didn't he know / I could swat his plane
from these skies like a gnat?'

The relationship lasted for twelve years or, perhaps more accurately,
the man survived for that length of time until he died. Queen Kong
grieved: 'I held him all night, shaking him / like a doll' (lines 71–2).
We are left with an **image** of a female wearing a man like a piece
of jewellery. Even if he is 'perfect, preserved', his eyes have been
replaced by 'tiny emeralds'. The penultimate stanza does, though,
suggest reciprocal tenderness between gorilla and man. Queen Kong
is left to experience loss, whereas the original story saw King Kong
killed.

This is one of the few **dramatic monologues** that present men in
anything like a positive light, but it should be noted that the man
involved is hardly able to offer any kind of resistance. A central
question to consider is whether this poem presents us with a power
shift from male to female or a recasting of a well-known **myth** from
a feminist point of view. Queen Kong clearly has some genuine
affection for the human male with whom she has had an intimate
relationship. The poem articulates a simultaneous sense of female

CONTEXT

Bloomingdale's
is a famous
department store
in New York.

 **CHECK
THE FILM**

The monster used
in making the film
King Kong was only
inches high, and the
sequences involving
the scene of King
Kong swatting
biplanes while on
top of the Empire
State Building were
achieved through
trick photography.

independence and an acknowledgement that the otherness of the
male can offer a worthwhile experience, however small. The
repetition of the adjective 'little' to describe the man's stature
and sexual organs could indicate endearment or a sense that he is
pleasantly non-threatening.

THE DEVIL'S WIFE

- The voice in this poem is that of Myra Hindley, one of the
  infamous Moors Murderers.
- The Devil is personified by her lover, the other convicted
  murderer, Ian Brady.
- The five parts of the poem chart variously her attraction to
  Brady, confession of further crimes, her religious conversion,
  the debate over whether she should be released and her musing
  upon the impact of her actions.

CONTEXT

Myra Hindley died
in Suffolk Prison
of natural causes
on 15 November
2002.

Brady and Hindley abducted, tortured and murdered four children.
Their bodies were dumped on Saddleworth Moor on the edge of the
Peak District outside Manchester. Brady murdered Edward Evans
(seventeen years old), John Kilbride (twelve years old) and Lesley
Ann Downey (ten years old). Hindley was jointly convicted for the
murder of Evans and Downey. She later confessed to the murders
of two other children, Keith Bennett (twelve years old) and Pauline
Reade (sixteen years old). One of the most appalling aspects of
their crime was the tape recording by the murderers of two of the
children's screams for mercy. They also photographed their victims.
In his youth, Brady had delighted in torturing small animals and,
later, children. Myra Hindley was sentenced to life imprisonment,
the judge stating that in her case life should mean that she stay in
prison for the rest of her days.

COMMENTARY

The first part of the poem, entitled 'Dirt', suggests the sort of
revelation made in a tabloid newspaper and also provides a

summary of the sort of people Brady and Hindley were. She became infatuated with this man who 'Looked at the girls / in the office as though they were dirt' (lines 2–3). The fascination that a bad person can have is authentically presented here: 'I gave / as good as I got till he asked me out' (lines 7–8). The man's physical aggression, 'He bit my breast' (line 10), and his insistence on her involvement in fetishistic ritual, 'he made me bury a doll' (line 12), is a disturbing prelude to even more sinister activity: 'looking at playgrounds, fairgrounds' (line 15) where children could be observed. The point at which sex between the man and woman first occurs, 'He entered me' (line 10), has a dual meaning in that the Devil possesses her spiritually too: 'I swooned in my soul' (line 11).

The picture conjured up of the Devil's wife at the end of part 1 is of a battered woman who learns to live with violence and becomes stone-hearted. Her 'Tongue of stone' and 'black slates / for eyes' suggest an unfeeling disposition and prepare for her presentation as Medusa in part 2. Being 'Nobody's Mam' will make maternal experience impossible. In the form of Medusa she returns to 'the wood where we'd buried / the doll'. The doll is an analogue of a murdered child and the repetitions of 'I know' show how guilty the woman is, but she tries to blame the Devil for her being what she is: 'He held my heart in his fist and he squeezed it dry' (line 24). The 'Medusa stare' that, as the Greek **myth** says, could turn living things to stone is an accurate description of Myra Hindley's expression in a famous photograph of her at the time of her conviction. In 'I didn't care' and 'It was nowt to me' we are confronted with the reality of a criminal who seemed utterly remorseless at the time. Carol Ann Duffy captures Hindley's north-western variety of English in 'Mam' and 'nowt', making it perfectly clear who Medusa represents in this section.

Her lack of concern turns to a realisation of the implications of what life imprisonment means, and the denials following in part 3 show her changing her story out of pure self-interest. Many people have taken Hindley's conversion to Catholicism as a convenient means of attempting to apply leverage in order to secure parole. She blamed Brady for leading her into bad ways and some influential people, most notably Lord Longford, believed her. The insistently

QUESTION

Compare the background presence of Myra Hindley and Ian Brady in 'In Mrs Tilscher's Class' (*The Other Country*) with Duffy's stark presentation of them in this poem.

CHECK THE NET

A BBC obituary of Hindley can be found by searching **http://news.bbc. co.uk** repetitive denials Duffy presents in the **sonnet** that forms part 3 suggest the mind of someone who is trying to shut out the reality of what she knows to be true or is so villainous that she will say anything to reduce her sentence by shifting the responsibility on to Brady. Duffy's choice of the sonnet form is inspired here, as a highly wrought form is ideally suited to presenting the crafty thinking of Hindley behind an apparently artless facility with language.

Section 4 suggests that the Devil's wife, who attempts not to 'Suffer', be considered a 'Monster' or to 'Burn in Hell', will confess in the morning of her 'fifty-year night'. In fact, Myra Hindley did confess in 1986 to two further murders. Public opinion did not soften, though, and she is still regarded by many as a 'Monster'. The use of the word 'Amen' which means 'so be it' is **ironic** in that it shows a wicked person appropriating the language of a benign discourse for her own ends.

 **CHECK THE BOOK**
The use of the word 'Amen' is reminiscent of the line in Shakespeare's *The Merchant of Venice*: 'The Devil can cite Scripture for his purpose' (I.3.96).

The concluding section presents a multiplicity of ways in which the woman might have been executed. The use of **anaphora** reinforces the nagging quality of the questions surrounding the capital punishment versus imprisonment debate in the first ten lines. The ten 'Ifs' are arrested by the single 'But' that begins the separated final two lines in which the Devil's wife (Hindley) asks what effect her crimes had on the national psyche and on herself. The fact that she uses the past tense – 'But what did I do to us all, to myself / When I was the Devil's wife?' – indicates that she claims to have changed.

In this poem Duffy confronts the perennial problem of the nature and source of evil. It is clear that there are certain individuals who seem to embody everything that we regard as malignant and repugnant and this is why Brady and Hindley are clearly interchangeable with the Devil and his wife in this finely imagined **dramatic monologue**. In deciding who would be the most likely wife for the Devil, Duffy chose Hindley on the basis of the crimes that left terrible psychological scars on families and the national consciousness. It is clear, too, that a woman is presented as being just as bad as any man.

FRAU FREUD

- The wife of the famous psychologist, Sigmund Freud, addressing a gathering of women, wearily lists synonyms for the word 'penis', drawing attention to the fact that she believes her husband's theories say far more about him than they do about anyone else.

COMMENTARY

The opening word – 'Ladies' – is unusual for the start of what is clearly a powerful feminist riposte to one of the most influential males of the twentieth century. Some women argue that its derivation from the Anglo-Saxon word meaning 'kneader of bread' is demeaning. Others would counter this by arguing that it places women at the heart of economic production. Whatever gloss a reader may wish to put on the word 'Ladies', it also signals an oratorical beginning such as might be expected at a lecture or convention. In this way, the wife of Freud is taking her place upon the lecturer's podium, the perfect location from which to debunk his theories.

Frau Freud emerges as a wholly reasonable woman who has 'no axe to grind' (line 10). Her continuation of the list of terms for penis indicates that she is tired of being tied to the discourse of a **phallocentric** society, the responsibility for the legitimising of which lies firmly at the door of her husband. She refutes any possible accusation that she might be a prude: 'I'm as au fait with Hunt-the-Salami / as Ms M. Lewinsky' (line 6).

Sigmund Freud (1856–1939) was perhaps the world's most famous psychologist. His analysis of human personality may be summarised thus: Phallic associated with the penis, Sapphic associated with the vagina. We have conscious and unconscious aspects of our personalities, and dreams are an expression of the way we suppress our neuroses, most of which are related to sexuality. Carol Ann Duffy wittily gives us Freud's wife's view of her husband's penis. She pities it. What she says here is a clever use

CONTEXT

Monica Lewinsky was a junior member of the White House staff, the details of whose sexual relationship with the US president Bill Clinton became public in 1998.

'FRAU FREUD' continued

of the psychoanalyst's technique. The whole of this man's theory that was to be taken so seriously by the world was based on no more than an obsession with phallic symbolism based on feelings of inadequacy about the size of his own penis. The plethora of synonyms for penis is an index of male obsession with this organ, not the female's.

In this instance Duffy's choice of the **sonnet** form presents a woman summarising a voluminous body of work by a man. In fourteen lines that include a large number of synonyms, Freud, and the manner in which his ideas may be reduced to a repetitive list, is **satirised**.

THE KRAY SISTERS

- The Kray sisters speak about their harsh upbringing and the affinity they feel with many of the strong women in history who promoted the feminist cause.

The voice in this poem is a composite one and could in some measure be considered a **dramatic monologue** as the two sisters speak as one throughout. This has the dual effect of making it unnecessary to tell separate stories and of presenting a united front against men that is intended to represent all women. The sisters speak predominantly in cockney rhyming **slang**, which has its roots in the **argot** of criminal fraternities in London. Felons would use rhyming slang as a code to outwit the police. The setting of the poem in the 1960s is consistent with the fact that the Kray twins operated their various illegal organisations around London at that time.

COMMENTARY

The first stanza outlines the reaction of men to the sisters, who deliberately have their suits tailored to accentuate their breasts. They display their 'thr'penny bits' (tits) with the help of clothes made in Savile Row, the street traditionally associated with male tailoring (line 4). Already, the reader is aware of a pair of women who like to steal a march on men. Their showbusiness connections are established in the use of the familiar 'Garland' (line 12). This, along with their visit to a club 'up West' and being used to 'bubbly, the best' (line 11), shows that they are wealthy and well connected.

In recounting the details of their childhood it is clear that they have a strong affinity with the suffragette movement through the influence of their grandmother, who was part of 'Emmeline's Army' (line 20) before the start of the First World War. It was the efforts of these women that led to the possibility of the sisters being what they are. Their grandmother reputedly 'knocked out' a horse with 'one punch', demonstrating an even more powerful response to male domination than that offered by Emily Davison, who was driven to throw herself under the king's horse at Epsom. This physical prowess made her famous on their 'manor' or territory. They learnt 'at her skirts' about the history of women's suffrage while 'inhaling the juniper fumes / of her Vera Lynn' (gin). They applaud the women of the past who secured the vote. The sisters' mother died giving birth to them and this makes them feel a link with all the other women who have suffered in the past.

This leads, in stanza 3, to their avowed shared sense of a 'vocation' to be in control of men. They 'wanted respect' for being able to shrivel 'a hard on with simply a menacing look' or double a man up with 'a knee in the orchestra stalls' (balls). Their vision of themselves and the future they desire is intimately bound up with their sense of connection with previous generations of women as they are presented 'holding the hand of the past' and assimilating (rather as taxi drivers gain 'the knowledge') 'the map of the city' under their feet. They become intimately familiar with the 'boozers', 'back alleys' and all other facets of their locale so as to be in a position to control it.

Stanzas 4 and 5 chart the development of the sisters from the 'soft' couple casually running the club called Ballbreakers to the gangsters running the 'gaff' called Prickteasers. They establish 'Protection' for women who seek it when 'in trouble' and this is diametrically opposed to the imposed 'protection' offered by the historical Kray

---

CONTEXT

The twins Ronnie and Reggie Kray were infamous, ruthless gangsters in the East End of London. Their empire spread to the west of London and included nightclubs, billiard halls and casinos. They were also involved in international fraud and were connected with the Mafia. Their organisation came to be known as 'the Firm'.

CONTEXT

As well as being involved in gangland murders, the Kray twins were friendly with celebrities such as the actresses Judy Garland (1922–69), Barbara Windsor (1937–) and Diana Dors (1931–84). During their trial, Ronnie famously said, 'If I wasn't here now I'd probably be having a drink with Judy Garland.'

CONTEXT

'Emmeline's Army' (line 20): Emmeline Pankhurst (1858–1928) spearheaded the women's suffrage movement in a forty-year crusade that culminated in the year of her death when British women were given the vote.

CONTEXT

Women were not given the right to vote in Britain until 1928, six years after their Irish counterparts.

CONTEXT

All the women listed in stanza 5 became famous in the 1960s (see the glossary for more details).

CONTEXT

'Vita and Violet' (line 35): Vita Sackville-West (1892–1962) was an English poet and novelist, and Violet Trefusis (1894–1972) was her love.

twins, who would stop at nothing if people refused their offer. They freely admit that the 'fruits / of feminism' made them 'rich, feared, famous, / friends of the stars' and go on to identify some of the stars in the constellation with which they are familiar. The list includes one of the leading feminists of the 1960s, Germaine Greer, and film stars such as Brigitte Bardot and Barbara Windsor. They claim to have received appreciative letters from women who felt safe under their protection. The implication here is that *'mugging old ladies'* and *'touching young girls'* have again become problems in society.

The final stanza articulates the sisters' desire to be remembered at their 'peak' and 'dressed to kill'. At the height of their power they 'leaned on Sinatra to sing for free'. Carol Ann Duffy creates a real sense of the impressiveness of this achievement since it is well known that Frank Sinatra had Mafia connections himself, emphasising the influence of the Krays. However, there is a feminist Trojan horse employed by Duffy as she reveals in the final four lines of the poem that the Sinatra in question is Nancy, the daughter of Frank. Her hit song, 'These Boots Are Made for Walking', is an anthem for the Kray sisters and women in general with its insistence on female power over the male. The words *'Are you ready, boots? Start walkin' …'* are a clarion call to women who are being urged to take control.

As a statement of the central tenets of what the Kray sisters believe, these words are memorable, but they are prefaced earlier on in the stanza with the clear indication that their influence is on the wane. What does this say for feminism in general? Is Duffy suggesting that certain battles may have been won but there is still a war that has to be prosecuted? Although the **tone** may verge on the comic at times, there are serious issues of sexual politics being raised as in so many of the poems in *The World's Wife*. If society does not, like the sisters, 'hear what's being said', then societal regression is all that can take place.

DEMETER

- Demeter describes the sadness and isolation of waiting for the return of Persephone.
- She rejoices in the return of the spring she brings with her.

COMMENTARY

Despite being the goddess of spring, Demeter has been disempowered since control over the seasons does not lie with her alone. This **sonnet** begins with bleak **images**, 'tough words' (line 3) that give way to more positive ones in the final tercet and **couplet**. Like the 'hard earth', 'granite' and 'flint', her heart feels cold and 'broken'. Demeter notices Persephone in what is presented like a long shot in a film. She is barely discernible but is recognisable 'at last' walking across fields. Her 'bare feet' indicate her affinity with the ground as well as acting as a sign that she has brought warmth and flowers back to melt the 'frozen lake' of her mother's heart. Demeter feels that the air has 'softened' just as the ice has melted.

There is a sense of expansiveness and joy conveyed through the open vowels in the **internal rhymes** of the fourth tercet; 'bare', 'swear' and 'air' when read aloud require expiration of air which ventilates the verse with the breath of spring. The **personification** of the 'smiling' sky is welcomed by Demeter as coming 'none too soon' and she is really imposing her feelings on nature. This use of **pathetic fallacy** is further developed in the tentative showing of 'the small shy mouth of a new moon', indicating that Demeter hardly dares believe that her daughter's return is real.

It is fitting that this poem should conclude *The World's Wife* since the personage of Demeter is independent of men and her most important relationship is with her daughter. The affinity she feels with the moon is directly linked to the female reproductive cycle and, as goddess of the spring, it is bound up with fertility and the hopeful prospect of new life. The mother–daughter relationship is central to many of the poems in this collection and it is the purity

> **CONTEXT**
>
> A tercet is a stanza or section of three lines.

CONTEXT

In Greek mythology Demeter was the goddess of the spring and mother of Persephone. Hades abducted Persephone and took her to the underworld. Demeter pleaded for her return and the god conceded that Persephone should spend half the year with him and half with her mother. This myth was used by the Greeks to explain the cycle of the seasons.

of love felt for Persephone by Demeter set against the selfish lust of Hades that places the **myth** at the heart of the debate surrounding sexual politics.

FEMININE GOSPELS

This collection, in common with *The World's Wife*, is written from a female perspective throughout, and focuses primarily upon the experience of women. However, unlike *The World's Wife*, the **dramatic monologue** is, apart from the poem 'Sub' (not included in *New Selected Poems 1984–2004*), replaced by narrative poems that seek to explore the truths of a variety of women's lives and stories ranging from Helen of Troy to Princess Diana.

There is no attempt in this collection to rewrite the four gospels of the New Testament; *Feminine Gospels* simply seeks to tell the truth about women's experience. In so far as the word gospel means 'good news', Duffy certainly does not present exclusively positive aspects of female experience. The collection is dedicated to men – her four brothers. This is enough to warn the reader not to adopt what could be a limited view of feminism, which, if its discourse is to be universally valid, needs to be inclusive of men but in a way that does not compromise itself. This is easier said than done, but such discourse cannot, of course, afford to fall into the trap of sexism that it accuses patriarchal discourse of peddling.

As in previous collections, Duffy places the marginalised centre stage and gives voice to the voiceless.

THE MAP-WOMAN

- A woman with a map for skin is described and her experiences explored.

This poem is an exploration of identity and a sense of self.

COMMENTARY

In stanza 1 we learn that what makes the woman distinctively herself has to be covered up with clothes. The long list of clothing items Duffy chooses to include draws attention to the fact that society tends to repress individuality, despite the fact that it could be argued that clothes also allow people to express it. Clothes, beyond preserving modesty, also mask the reality of the nakedness beneath. The way we dress ourselves is representative of the ways in which we conform to or deviate from expected norms.

Irrespective of our experiences throughout life, we carry memory with us, the map of where we came from. The map on the woman's skin is a 'birthmark, tattoo' (line 7). Just like a map, our formative experiences give us reference points to which we are able to return, 'a precis of where to end or go back or begin' (line 10). A map can give information about topography, location and settlement.

By exploring the map on the woman's skin through her own intimate knowledge of it, we are taken on a simultaneous tour of her life and that of the town's. This poem is therefore about a sense of place both in literal and **metaphorical** ways. The intimacy of the woman's knowledge of her own body gives a sense of the intimacy with which she knows her home town: 'Over her breast was the heart of the town' (line 11) and 'She knew / if you crossed the bridge at her nipple ... like old print / on a page' (lines 16–23) are clear examples of this.

A striking feature of the poem is Duffy's shifts in perspective that correspond to zooming in and out or changing the scale of the map. Sometimes she chooses to show us close-up details and sometimes a sweeping overview. This metaphor for identity, a sense of self and place, is linked to the same sense of place explored in 'Originally' (*The Other Country*).

CONTEXT

Like the stories in the gospels, the poems in this collection may be read as parables.

BEAUTIFUL

- The lives of four famous beautiful women are reflected upon in such a way as to focus upon the fact that being beautiful can often be fatal, not just for those who are captivated by such beauty but also for those who possess it.

CONTEXT

Princess Diana was killed in a car crash on 31 August 1997 in Paris after the Mercedes in which she was travelling with her lover, Dodi Al Fayed, went out of control in a subway.

The four sections of this poem examine the lives of Helen of Troy, Cleopatra, Marilyn Monroe and Princess Diana. Significantly, the two women of antiquity were powerful, whereas the iconic beauties of the twentieth century, Marilyn Monroe and Princess Diana, were victims, both dying in tragic circumstances.

COMMENTARY

Helen of Troy was born from an egg produced as a result of the rape of Leda by Zeus, who took, on that occasion, the form of a swan: 'She was born from an egg, / a daughter of the gods' (stanza 1). When Paris abducted Helen, her husband Menelaus launched a thousand ships and sailed for Troy to bring her back. The ensuing Trojan War led to the slaughter of many: 'A thousand ships – / on every one a thousand men' (lines 26–7). The power of Helen's attraction is emphasised through Duffy's presentation of the men who had 'her name tattooed / upon the muscle of his arm' (lines 31–2). She is described as 'a princess with the common touch, / queen of his heart, pin-up, superstar'. This neatly conveys to a modern audience that Helen of Troy was the ancient equivalent of Princess Diana, who was known as 'the people's princess' and wanted, in her own words, to be 'the queen of hearts'.

Helen's orgasmic cries 'like the bird of calamity's' signal the reality that there will be a long-term price to pay for short-term gratification, but do not immediately result in catastrophe as the young Trojan men 'marched now to the syllables of her name' (stanza 5). The next stanza begins with 'Beauty is fame', a statement that reminds us that all four women presented in the poem were famous for their beauty but paid a high price. This is made plain in the fourth section about Princess Diana: 'Beauty is fate.' The remainder of this section of the poem deals with the speculation about the fate of Helen after the Greeks came to claim her back; its conclusion presents her maid as the most loyal person in Helen's life, who maintains her mistress's mystery. This is neatly expressed in what can be read as a **metaphor**: 'But lived alone / and kept a little bird inside a cage.' The true story of Helen is kept locked up in the cage of her servant's memory.

The second section of the poem presents Cleopatra, queen of Egypt, who famously enslaved the Roman triumvir Mark Antony to her love. She is a woman who can more than match men in drinking, sexual appetite and acumen. She may be summed up in 'Tough beauty.' Cleopatra's power is emphasised in such details as: 'She … slipped her gambling hand / into his pouch and took his gold, bit it, / Caesar's head between her teeth' and 'she lay above him … her powder blushing on his stubble'. She matches Antony 'in drinking games … until the big man slid beneath the table, wrecked.' Her influence is further emphasised as we are told that Antony 'had no choice, upped sticks, / downed tools, went back with her' after Cleopatra had followed him, dressed as a boy, and 'made him fuck her as a lad'. Her sexually omnivorous nature is emphasised here, along with the fact that Antony was unable to resist her. The fusion of the political, the personal and the fatal is summarised by the conclusion of the section, as the couple, though reunited, must face the reality 'of armies changing sides, / of cities lost forever in the sea, of snakes'. These lines refer to details of Shakespeare's play. Antony is dismayed to see the Egyptian fleet surrendering off Alexandria. Cleopatra flees to her monument and has it put about that she is dead. Antony, believing the rumour, kills himself. To avoid capture by Octavius, Cleopatra clasps an asp to her bosom and another to her arm. So Eros and Thanatos are, as in the case of all four women in this poem, inextricably linked.

The third part focuses on Marilyn Monroe, the fêted and fated film actress. She had a difficult early life and had a sequence of marriages and affairs. In an **image** that links the Greek ideals of physical perfection and the attractions of twentieth-century Aphrodite, Duffy focuses on Monroe's second husband, the baseball player Joe DiMaggio (1914–): 'An athlete / licked the raindrops from her

CHECK THE BOOK

Antony is referred to in Shakespeare's play *Antony and Cleopatra* as 'The triple pillar of the world' (I.1.12), while Enobarbus speaks of Cleopatra's 'infinite variety' (II.2.246).

CONTEXT

Eros was the Greek god of sexual love; Thanatos was the god of death.

'BEAUTIFUL' continued

CONTEXT

John F. Kennedy
was assassinated
on 22 November
1963 in Dallas,
Texas. Marilyn
Monroe died on
5 August 1962.

 **CHECK
THE NET**
An interesting BBC
site relating to
Marilyn Monroe
can be found at
**http://news.bbc.
co.uk/onthisday**

fingertips / to quench his thirst.' The other man Duffy alludes to in
'A poet came, / found her wondrous to behold' is the playwright
Arthur Miller (1915–), Monroe's third husband. The third stanza
of this section presents details relating to Monroe's decline, and her
dependence on drugs and alcohol. Monroe famously sang, as the
penultimate stanza of this section reminds us, '*Happy / Birthday to
you. Happy Birthday, Mr President*' to John F. Kennedy in 1962 and
gave him a Rolex watch. He ordered one of his aides to 'get rid of
it'. Her performance was viewed by some as evidence of a romantic
link with Kennedy. Certainly, 'Somebody big was watching her'.

After the glamour of a film-star life came the sad death of Monroe
the icon. In the final stanza of this third section, Duffy presents the
ironic tension between the truth that Hollywood simultaneously
helped to kill and immortalise Marilyn Monroe. Although she was
at an incredibly low ebb in 1962, 'They filmed on, deep, dumped
what they couldn't use / on the cutting-room floor'. The
Hollywood juggernaut is conveyed in the urgency of the rhythm
of the verse and its terse presentation of a director's instructions:
'action, cut, quiet please, action, cut, quiet please / action, cut'.
In helping to hasten her end, they simultaneously ensured that
her memory lived on, 'till she couldn't die when she died'. The
undignified death of Monroe is recalled at the conclusion of the
section as we are reminded that she was discovered naked on her
bed. Tellingly, Duffy chooses to remind us that the woman who
was once the world's most famous sex symbol was reduced to a sex
object. The indifference of the 'smoking cop who watched / as they
zipped her into the body-bag' is leavened by the fact that he saw her
exposed as she really was, 'noticed / her strong resemblance to
herself, the dark roots / of her pubic hair'. The details associated
with identity, image and sexuality crystallise the issues relating to
what many believe was the suicide of Marilyn Monroe. Her pubic
hair having dark roots obviously suggests that she was not a 'natural
blonde' and that her dyeing was intimately linked to her dying,
since she had to hide behind an 'eye-mask' and make-up applied by
a maid who 'painted the beauty on in khaki, / pinks, blues'. The
colours here suggest both childish primaries but also military
camouflage – all of them part of the mask Monroe hid behind.

The final section of the poem is concerned with the death of Diana, Princess of Wales. Duffy begins Diana's story with the matter-of-fact 'Dead'. The use of the present tense in the opening stanza serves to reinforce the reality of the death of the princess. The descriptive detail in the remainder of the stanza presents a composite of what Diana was in life and how she was in death, in her coffin. She was 'elegant' but became 'elegant bone / in mud', reminding us that mortality unites us all and reunites us with earth. The noun/verb combinations of 'ankles crossed, / knees clamped, hands clasped' signal a contrast between her openness in general and sexual terms in life, and the chaste, prayerful suggestion of the words 'clamped' and 'clasped'. There is also, though, a sense that natural impulse has been unnaturally curtailed and restricted. The idea that she has an 'empty head' relates to the reality that a dead person's brain precludes thought, but also to the idea that Princess Diana was never regarded as having intellectual prowess. In this sense she was categorised as a 'dumb blonde' in much the same way as Marilyn Monroe was.

The second and third stanzas focus on the influence of Diana on 'Plain women' who tried to be like her in all respects. Stanza 4 hints at her mortality while celebrating her beauty 'as her bones danced / in a golden dress in the arms / of her wooden prince'. The enjambed link between stanzas 4 and 5 recalls the irony of the situation where the person considered at the time to be the world's most beautiful woman, and certainly the most photographed, 'posed alone / in front of the Taj Mahal, / betrayed, beautifully pale'. The Prince of Wales had, since the beginning of his marriage, been having an affair with Camilla Parker Bowles; this explains why Duffy presents the princess as 'betrayed'. Diana, the Roman goddess of the hunt, was also associated with the moon, which is 'beautifully pale' like a blonde woman.

The sixth stanza presents the reality that the icon who was known for her love/hate relationship with the press was treated with contempt by that which was largely kept in business by reporting her every move. A story featuring Diana would guarantee massive sales for the tabloids. The brutality of the italicised words of the journalists emphasises that 'they loved her' for purely mercenary reasons. '*Act like a fucking princess*' and '*Give us a smile, cunt*' convey the utter contempt and dirty-mindedness of the average hack. The sector of the press that thrives on salaciousness has no difficulty in reducing a woman to a crude term for one of her sexual parts. The disturbing extra implication, though, is that the press could be seen as part of the establishment that appropriated and used Diana as a means of perpetuating itself.

> **CONTEXT**
>
> Earl Spencer, Princess Diana's brother, said in his eulogy at Westminster Abbey that he thought it ironic his sister was named after the Roman goddess of the hunt when she was hunted all her life by the press.

As in life, Princess Diana was linked in death with Marilyn Monroe, when the pop star Elton John sang a hastily rewritten Bernie Taupin lyric to their song 'Candle in the Wind' at her funeral in Westminster Abbey. The song had originally been written in memory of Monroe. The opening of the original version is 'Goodbye, Norma Jean', while the rewritten version begins 'Goodbye, England's rose'. Interestingly, the first version insists on celebrating the true identity of Marilyn Monroe (her real name was Norma Jean Baker) that lay behind her iconic public persona, while preserving Diana Spencer's iconic status as the embodiment of English female beauty through the metaphorical use of a rose.

The final stanza is a bitter reflection upon what Duffy surely sees as the hypocrisy of a nation that was part of a seedy feeding frenzy, colluding with the pursuit of a beautiful, good-natured woman by unscrupulous journalists but who lined the streets with themselves and 'acres of flowers'. The final line – 'History's stinking breath in her face' – contrasts Diana's implied purity with the corruption of at least a sector of a nation that many believe treated her shabbily.

THE DIET

- A woman diets with sad effects.

Duffy plays with the idea that inside every fat person there is a thin one waiting to get out, but inverts it in the conclusion of the poem: 'inside the Fat Woman now, / trying to get out'.

COMMENTARY

The narrative in the poem is cyclical. First, the woman's self-denial is catalogued: 'No sugar, / salt, dairy, fat, protein, starch or alcohol' (stanza 1), and this is contrasted with her desire in stanza 8 to return to self-indulgence:

> Then it was sweet. Then it was Stilton,
> Roquefort, weisslacker-kase, gex; it was smoked salmon
> with scrambled eggs …

Tragically, though, she cannot enjoy her former gastronomic pleasures because she has become so small. This locking out from the life she once knew is presented through a fairy-tale-like transformation by Duffy, who then shows us that the woman is a victim of what becomes a nightmare for her. There is a clear connection with *Alice's Adventures in Wonderland* as the woman shrinks to 'the height of a thimble' (stanza 3). However, unlike Alice, she will not return to her old self. From becoming 'Anorexia's true daughter' (stanza 3) she moves on to be 'Seed small' (stanza 4) and 'lay in the tent of a nostril like a germ' (stanza 6). There are some Swiftian, scatological **images** in the sixth stanza that clearly engage with the revulsion many have for obesity but also for the body in general. Duffy concentrates on the nooks and crannies of the body where germs breed. The woman is tiny but could be a hippopotamus as she 'wallowed / in mud under fingernails'. This neatly prepares the reader for the end of the poem, which leaves us with the surprising image of the real person being trapped inside the person she has become. Being hit by an 'avalanche' (stanza 7) of food after being swallowed by someone, the woman who once ate everything is left unable to eat anything herself. It is clear that Duffy is reflecting upon the idea that in conforming to what society seems to demand of people in terms of body shape, unhappiness can result.

The fairy-tale element takes us to a fantastical world, but we cannot forget that the dwindling of the self is something that is very real for people struggling with their size, body image and psychological well-being. Sometimes we make decisions and follow a course of action that we end up regretting for the rest of our lives.

CHECK THE BOOK

Lewis Carroll's *Alice's Adventures in Wonderland* (1865) and its sequel, *Through the Looking-Glass* (1872), quickly became classics.

CHECK THE BOOK

At one point in Jonathan Swift's *Gulliver's Travels* (1726), during his voyage to Brobdingnag, Lemuel Gulliver comments: 'There was a woman with a cancer in her breast, swelled to a monstrous size, full of holes, in two or three of which I could have easily crept, and covered my whole body.' The ratio of Gulliver's size to that of the Brobdingnagians is one to twelve.

ANON

- The effacement of women in life is presented through the idea that so many of them have remained anonymous.

COMMENTARY

CONTEXT

The poet and critic Sean O'Brien commented in the *Sunday Times* that 'Poetry, like love, depends on a kind of recognition ... [Duffy] could well become the representative poet of the present day.'

This short poem connects *Feminine Gospels* very closely to *The World's Wife* in that it helps to provide what might reasonably be seen as an insight into both collections as 'projects'. *The World's Wife* gives voice to the many women in history who have become anonymous and unconsidered by having famous husbands, while *Feminine Gospels* seeks to narrate female experience in ways that make permanent the truth of that experience and to make clear that to be a 'nurse, a nanny, / maybe a nun' (stanza 1) might as far as most are concerned mean they are 'Anon'. Women are naturally caring and men have exploited this. The single vowel difference between 'a nun' and 'Anon' reminds us that some women choose to be anonymous, but this does not mean that we should forget their contribution. Stanza 2 deals with the reality that some women abandon ambition and convince themselves that they are fulfilled as 'Anon' having 'packed it all in, / the best verb, the right noun'. Duffy focuses on the tools of her own trade to highlight the way in which the quest for excellence can be abandoned. The **metaphorical** use of 'verb' and 'noun' reminds us that we can be tempted to settle for second best. In an **image** that reminds us of one of her earlier poems, 'Small Female Skull', Duffy writes of a woman who 'kept her skull / on a shelf in a room – / Anon's' (stanza 3). This image conjures the idea of a living death, as well as defying reality. The woman's insistence that her skull 'cleared its throat / as though it had something / to get off its chest' is an insightful comment about how people who feel they are unrecognised crave acknowledgement. Whoever the anonymous woman is (introduced in the subjunctive in the first line of the poem), she has not asserted herself but has 'passed on her pen / like a baton / down through the years' (stanza 4). Duffy shows her appreciation of all the anonymous women in history who made real contributions by bearing witness to them in writing *Feminine Gospels*, and the cover-breaking modulation from the third to the first person in the opening of the final stanza – 'But I know best' – is a statement that could be a byline for the entire collection.

THE LIGHT GATHERER

- The poet reflects upon her daughter as a source of light and love.

This poem was written for Carol Ann Duffy's daughter and recalls her birth and growing up into a young child intoxicated with the possibilities of life and language.

COMMENTARY

The parent is struck by the wonder of her child, who seems to have arrived in her life in some miraculous way: 'You fell from a star / into my lap' (lines 19–20). Feelings of awe, reverence, fascination and, above all, love are presented in a variety of **images** associated with light. The luminescence of a baby's skin is captured in 'your cupped palms / each held a candlesworth under the skin' (stanza 1). The interior light that shines from a child is captured through the **internal rhyme** of 'and as you grew / light gathered in you' (stanza 2). There is a 'light of a smile' (stanza 3), and 'kissed feet' that 'glowed' (stanza 4). The poet 'knelt watching' (stanza 6) her daughter as she slept, an image that clearly conveys reverence. The sequence of light images in the poem is not difficult to follow. The reader should be aware in the case of this poem that it is one that safely allows us to read the 'I' of the poem as that of the poet herself.

The conclusion of the poem that contemplates the future as 'a tunnel of years' captures every parent's sense that the loved child will one day have a life of its own. This beautiful poem dwells on the purity of uncomplicated and unconditional love that is a constant source of light. The child gathers light to herself but also garners it for the parent, who is bathed in its beneficent reflection.

 QUESTION

Trace the light imagery in the poem and examine what it reveals about the poet's feelings as her daughter grows up.

NORTH-WEST

- A ride on a Mersey ferry leads the poet to contemplation upon direction, place and time.

CONTEXT

This sonnet was featured on National Poetry Day in October 2000. Poets were asked to contribute a sonnet based on a point of the compass or a wind rose, a diagram showing the relative frequency of wind directions at a place.

Duffy's choice of title is doubly appropriate since it signals both a point on the compass and a geographical region of England, with a specific focus on Liverpool. This area has both national cultural significance and personal resonance for Duffy, Liverpool being the city where she studied philosophy at university and where she had a long friendship with the poet Adrian Henri.

COMMENTARY

There is a rather melancholy **tone** in this poem that verges on the elegiac. This sonnet is written in rhyming and half-rhyming **couplets**. **Half-rhyme** or pararhyme is often used to introduce what amounts to the equivalent of a minor key in music. Funeral music is often written in a minor key. The mood of the poem is established in the first sentence, as the **persona**, addressing someone else (presumably the dedicatee), says:

> However it is we return to the water's edge
> where the ferry grieves down by the Pier Head,
> we do what we always did and get on board.

Two friends return to their youth through the ferry ride, and experience an aching sense of loss. Like Liverpool that 'drifts out of reach' (line 4), their youth has receded, but their shared memory of old haunts and experiences is individual to them, 'the place no map / or heritage guide can reveal'. The river, **symbol** of flux and change, is still the river that ran in the years of their youth. The fixing of a point, 'an X on a wave / marks the spot', is an expression of how we take our past back to a place we knew intimately and, in what amounts to a ritualistic act, bury – or in this case drown – it in the Mersey that becomes 'a grave / for our ruined loves, unborn children, ghosts' (lines 8–9). The rhyme of 'wave' and 'grave' brings water, something normally aligned with life, as a locus for death.

The Mersey sustained shipping and industry for centuries but its docks are now lined with flats. The old Liverpool is indeed 'out of reach'. The **volta** or turn in this sonnet is delayed until line 10 as the friends 'look back at the skyline'. We can all feel that the city in which we lived, studied, worked or loved no longer belongs to us, and that we are no different from the tourist, anonymous where we were once recognised and integral to at least part of the city's life and culture. This idea is clearly conveyed in lines 10–12. The first sentence of the final couplet links the gulls' cry of '*yeah yeah yeah*', a quotation from the chorus of the Beatles' song 'She Loves You', to the 'huge silvery bird, / a kiss on the lip of the wind' in lines 4–5. The final line – 'Frets of light on the river. Tearful air' – juxtaposes the excitement of past youth in the city where popular music took off in the early 1960s with the mournful present, as the sky cries its rain. Duffy brilliantly plays on the **ambiguity** of the word 'Frets' at the start of the final line, as it suggests both bands of light on the Mersey, turning it imaginatively into a massive guitar neck – a bright reminder of the city's musical energy – and also multiple worries made visible. In short, this sonnet mixes memory and the confounding of desire.

DEATH AND THE MOON

- This is an elegy commemorating the poet Adrian Henri and is dedicated to his widow.

The indifference of the moon to the death of people is reflected upon in this bleak poem, as well as the terrible feeling of loss that bereavement brings.

COMMENTARY

Duffy examines the familiar sensation we all feel that we could almost reach out and touch the moon when it appears huge in the sky at certain times. Rationally, we know that it is almost a quarter of a million miles away, but we nonetheless find ourselves preferring to believe in the possibility of doing what we clearly cannot. She

> **CONTEXT**
>
> Adrian Henri (born in 1932) died in Liverpool on 21 December 2000.

explores our sense of distance in a literal, physical and measurable way and then considers this alongside that which we find incomprehensible and immeasurable. The opening of the poem makes this clear:

> The moon is nearer than where death took you
> at the end of the old year. Cold as cash
> in the sky's dark pocket, its hard old face
> is gold as a mask tonight.

The **internal rhyme** of 'old', 'Cold' and 'gold' and the alliterated 'd' emphasise the hard reality of death. Beyond the visual **image** of a bright coin against a dark background, the language used by Duffy presents the sky as keeping a cold coin in its pocket to convey the coldness of death and the idea that we are all small change in the context of time. The moon's face is 'hard' like coins but the primary suggestion is that the moon is unmoved by the 'widow's unbearable cry' (line 16).

The conversational **tone** of the poem is consistent throughout, addressing the deceased in a way that employs domestic details that might well be familiar to the friend being addressed. The goldfish in the pond become 'tongues' (stanza 3) that serve to speak for the speaker, who seems lost for words. This contrasts with the vastness of the 'black night' that is 'mute'. Lines 6–7 – 'the ghosts of my wordless breath reach / for the stars' – convey both the image of visible breath on a cold night but also a desire to transcend language in order to achieve spiritual union, or something like it, with the lost friend. This union can happen in memory, of course.

The second stanza, at the centre of the poem, recalls the funeral. The 'lip of your open grave' prepares us through the image of the boundary of the mouth for the reliving of the experience through a haunting dream: 'the ground gulped you, swallowed you whole' (line 14). Throwing earth onto a coffin is a familiar ritual designed to remind us of mortality, a means of saying goodbye without words, a concrete code. The handful of earth is 'tough confetti' that 'stuttered / like morse', highlighting the fact that this rite of passage is sad, unlike a marriage, and that all the bereaved friend wants to say is articulated through the sound of earth pattering on the coffin lid.

The speaker in the poem speculates upon the nature of death and where we go, if anywhere, after death. The dead friend is 'Unreachable' and 'Unseeable'; the cry of the dead man's widow 'unbearable'. Not even poems can reach the dead friend, who was a poet himself. It seems that 'Unreachable / by prayer' is a statement that says prayer itself is futile because there is nothing beyond death. Duffy concludes by observing: 'The black night / is huge, mute, and you are further forever than that.' Here, infinity lies in the irrevocable fact of death, not in the hope of everlasting life.

> **CONTEXT**
>
> Samuel Morse invented a code that turned each letter of the alphabet into a series of dots and dashes, allowing letters to be sent as short electrical signals. The most famous example is · · · – – – · · · which decodes to SOS – save our souls.

EXTENDED COMMENTARIES

TEXT 1 – THE GRAMMAR OF LIGHT (*MEAN TIME*)

Even barely enough light to find a mouth,
and bless both with a meaningless O, teaches,
spells out. The way a curtain opened at night
lets in neon, or moon, or a car's hasty glance,
and paints for a moment someone you love, pierces.   5

And so many mornings to learn; some
when the day is wrung from damp, grey skies
and rooms come on for breakfast
in the town you are leaving early. The way
a wasteground weeps glass tears at the end of a street.   10

Some fluent, showing you how the trees
in the square think in birds, telepathise. The way
the waiter balances light in his hands, the coins
in his pocket silver, and a young bell shines
in its white tower ready to tell.   15

Even a saucer of rain in a garden at evening
speaks to the eye. Like the little fires
from allotments, undressing in veils of mauve smoke
as you walk home under the muted lamps,
perplexed. The way the shy stars go stuttering on.   20

And at midnight, a candle next to the wine
slurs its soft wax, flatters. Shadows
circle the table. The way all faces blur
to dreams of themselves held in the eyes.
The flare of another match. The way everything dies. 25

In this poem from *Mean Time*, the poet presents light, in place of words, as a means of ordering experience. In doing so she draws attention to some of the collection's most important preoccupations. The effects of time, the function of memory and the limitations of words are all engaged with in an ingenious encoding of experience through light. The medium of words is notoriously opaque and it is this opacity that Carol Ann Duffy deals with in this and other poems such as 'River' and 'Words, Wide Night' (*The Other Country*).

www. CHECK THE NET

For a comprehensive list of Duffy's work, including her poetry collections for children, search **http://www. contemporary writers.com**

If we remember that grammar is a term used in two distinct ways by linguists then we will be able to address what seems to be at the centre of Duffy's concerns. Grammar may be viewed in prescriptive or descriptive terms. Most people see grammar as consisting of rules that need to be learnt. Modern linguists, though, adopt a descriptive approach, preferring to categorise language on the basis of how it is used; they do not seek to be arbiters of correctness. Duffy concentrates on both the prescriptive model in which there are 'so many mornings to learn' and the descriptive in that she is very observational concerning the way light makes sense of things.

The poem begins with the **image** of a night-time kiss. The 'meaningless O' is the shape of the mouths as they kiss, but the light that enabled the lovers to find each other is not meaningless, it 'teaches, / spells out'. Already words as a means of exploring the world are being replaced. Light 'paints' a person. Of course they are already there, but the beholder is only able to see as a result of illumination. Illumination is presented in both a literal and **metaphorical** sense as the term is associated with understanding. In the case of the loved one in the first stanza such illumination as there is only lasts for 'a moment'. The **personification** of the car with its 'hasty glance' emphasises this. The closeness of sound between 'neon' and 'moon' emphasises that both can provide a glimpse of a lover which 'pierces', despite the fact that one is a natural source of light and the other artificial.

There is a real sense of difficulty communicated at the opening of the second stanza. Each morning is different and its effects of light need to be learnt like the rules of grammar. The first morning mentioned is presented metaphorically as one which has been 'wrung from damp, grey skies' like a rather overused dishcloth. Duffy captures the atmosphere of such a morning when one rises early enough to see lights being switched on in people's houses as one leaves town early. The personification of the 'wasteground' that 'weeps glass tears at the end of a street' is almost surreal and the lighting effect, to this reader, is redolent of a Magritte sky in which there are elements of both night-time and daytime lighting. Rain is suggested by 'weeps' but light reflected off broken glass may be implied.

QUESTION

Compare 'The Grammar of Light' with 'Away and See' and 'Nostalgia' (*Mean Time*), focusing upon the ways in which Duffy addresses the problem of language as a system of signification.

Duffy deliberately uses linguistic terms and applies them to her imaginary grammar of light. Mornings are described as 'fluent' at the beginning of stanza 3. This word is linked to another surreal image, that of trees thinking 'in birds'. The birds' song is obviously only audible but Duffy draws attention to the fact that light allows us to see the source of the sound which she imagines might be the thoughts of trees that usually 'telepathise'. This is another crucial word as it refers to the ability to communicate without language, something that the poem claims for light. Another visual observation is presented through the playing of light on glasses carried on a tray by a waiter who 'balances light in his hands'. He does not balance the light but the tray, of course; the poet is reminding us that we could not make such an observation without the light to make sense of the situation. Added to this, we *could* not say that he has 'silver' coins in his pocket. We need not go much further here but might consider what we could say without light. By considering the way we make sense of things through the visual, Duffy is engaging in one of her familiar preoccupations, the testing of the limitations of language. We are told in stanza 3 that a bell 'shines', a verb enacting its visual being and one that significantly precedes its expected primary function. The fact that it is 'ready to tell' may be **ambiguous** as it could simply be saying that it is there because we are able to perceive it as such. We think of the 'toll' of a bell so the poet is again drawing parallels between what we see and what we articulate and how both relate to a decoding process. A saucer 'speaks to the eye', a deft presentation of light as language. The visual and linguistic are linked. The 'shy stars go stuttering on' (stanza 4), indicating difficulty in articulation but also reminding us of the way the light we perceive coming from stars is intermittent at times, and leads us to claim that they twinkle. The final stanza's presentation of what could well be a romantic dinner for two uses the word 'slurs' to suggest the fluidity of wax as it runs down a candle but also conveys the effect of wine on speech. As a source of light itself, it 'flatters' – a well-known effect. The 'Shadows' that 'circle the table' are not unexpected in the subdued lighting of a restaurant at midnight but there is quite a sinister sense that darkness threatens. This is certainly borne out in the final image of death in the last line of the poem. The visual effect created by the word 'blur' is, in the grammar of light, equivalent to 'slurs' in the grammar of words. This ingenious rhyme draws the reader's attention to the way in which Duffy has been at pains to reinterpret experience through the medium of the visual. The 'flare' of a match lasts, like the glimpses of the lover in stanza 1, only for 'a moment'.

The visual element concentrated on by Duffy is almost painterly, and this poem might easily be viewed as chiaroscuro in words, a term from painting which is concerned with the effects created by light and shade. The scenes depicted could easily be viewed as a sequence of paintings, ranging from the purely representational to the surreal. This is something of a translation from one language medium to another.

In order to make sense of this poem it is necessary to establish that it is about how we are able to make sense of the world. When we learn grammar in the conventional sense we need to learn its rules so that we are able to categorise our experience in words. There is a distinct sequence of words associated with language but they are transferred to light in 'so many mornings to learn'.

The manner in which Duffy uses light as a means of testing experience may be related to the manner in which Ludwig

CHECK THE NET

Search the Internet for a discussion of Wittgenstein's concept of a language game.

Wittgenstein, one of her favourite philosophers, viewed language. A detailed discussion of his ideas is not within the scope of these Notes, but it is useful to mention that the central questions of his *Tractatus* are: How is language possible? How can anyone, by uttering a sequence of words, say something? And how can another person understand them? His solution was that a sentence that says something (a proposition) must be 'a picture of reality'; it must show a situation in the world. His picture theory seemed to explain the 'connection between the signs on paper and a situation outside in the world'. Duffy is viewing presenting light as something that literally does paint pictures of reality.

One of the most striking features of the *Tractatus* is its conception of how the limits of language correspond with the limits of thought. His later *Investigations* posited the idea that language may be viewed rather like a game whose rules we must learn. This again links with 'And so many mornings to learn' in stanza 2. Ultimately, the signifying power of language is somehow required to live up to the task of articulating that which is beyond itself.

The overall impression created in this poem is one of negation and pessimism, largely as a result of the force of its last sentence. Despite the flaring of matches and the playing of light in various places, there is no real illumination in the sense of visionary insight. All remains externally observed and detached. We might view the poem, then, as one that both celebrates variegation and contemplates mortality. Certainly, annihilation is pointed to in 'The way everything dies.'

> **CONTEXT**
>
> 'Words, Wide Night' from *The Other Country* is another poem in which Duffy ponders the limitations of words.

TEXT 2 – PLUTO (*MEAN TIME*)

When I awoke
a brand new planet
Had been given a name –

    this Home I'm in,
    it has the same soap suddenly;   5
    so, washing my hands,
    I'm thinking *Pluto Pluto Pluto*,
    thrilled,
    beside myself.

CONTEXT

Pluto was
discovered in 1930
by Clyde W.
Tombaugh.

And then I notice things;   10
brown coins of age on my face the size of ha'pennies.
An hourglass weeping the future into the past

– and I was a boy.

I cry out now in my bath,
shocked and bereaved again   15
by not quite seeing us all,
half-hearing my father's laugh –
without the help and support of the woman I love.

Tangerine soap.
To think of another world out there   20
in the dark,
unreachable,
of what it was like.

In this poem from *Mean Time*, a man in an old people's home
looks back on his childhood and, particularly, remembers the
discovery of the planet Pluto, an event that coincided with the
day he was born.

The **persona** in 'Pluto', another of Duffy's **dramatic monologues**,
is transported back in time by the most evocative of our senses:
smell. As an adult living in a 'Home' he is reminded by the scent
of 'Tangerine soap' of a different, childhood home where he felt
safe with his parents. The institutionalised man yearns for an
uncomplicated childhood past. We discover that he has had to come
to terms with the death of both his parents and the poem finishes
with him making an apparently simple statement about the memory
of 'another world out there', the planet Pluto being discovered and
the excitement surrounding the event.

As the title suggests, this poem is partly concerned with the
outermost planet in our solar system. The opening of the poem
recalls a time of intense, youthful optimism and excitement when,
as a child, the man remembers the naming of a new planet. The boy
wakes to find that 'a brand new planet / had been given a name'
(lines 2–3). The naivety of this view is disarming but incorrect

nonetheless. The planet is not brand new but has been in existence for a very long time. It seems, though, that the very act of naming calls Pluto into existence in the mind of the boy. This is reminiscent of Adam in the Bible naming things. It also relates to the theory of language that posits the idea of existence only being possible within its own frame of reference. The boy repeats the name of the 'brand new' planet like an incantation, a form of words that seems to have almost magical properties: '*Pluto Pluto Pluto*' (line 7).

There are other discoveries going on in the poem, too. There is a clear correspondence between the discovery being made by an astronomer and the feelings of hope and discovery in a young life. We are also reminded of the fact that inside every adult is a child. We may view these complexities in terms of relative distances. Pluto is the most distant of the planets from the sun, the source of all life on earth. By analogy, the 'unreachable' planet becomes symbolic of the way in which the man's life as a boy and the lives of his parents are unreachable. The outer limits of the solar system were redefined in 1930, just as the outer limits of the man's experience are redefined as he grows older. His childhood now seems as distant to him as the planet Pluto and this adds to the poignancy of the poem's last line. He may move imaginatively into another temporal orbit but his desire to relive 'what it was like' to be a secure child is confounded by the very process of time itself. This leads us to revisit one of Duffy's major preoccupations in this collection, the effects of time.

In simple terms we see that a boy has become a man. He notices 'brown coins of age' on his face. The fact that they are 'the size of ha'pennies' dates him in a previous era. Duffy's complex treatment of time is important. The tenses of the verbs represent the oscillation between the persona's younger and older selves. The poem begins in the past tense and we realise that even this has two possible perspectives. One of these is the older man remembering the discovery of Pluto a long time previously, and the other is the voice of the persona as a boy speaking of a very recent past. In this way we become aware of an almost concentric model of time, rather like the orbits of planets as represented in atlases. Another analogy might be that of a Russian doll. Such ideas lead us to consider the

> **CONTEXT**
>
> British coinage was decimalised in February 1971, but before that had been more or less unchanged since the latter half of the seventeenth century.

direct confrontation of time in the striking image of 'An hour glass weeping the future into the past' (line 12). This poignantly summarises the predicament of all human beings and the way they are defined by time and are victims of its unceasing passage. The grains of sand become tears mourning their very fall. The upper portion of the hourglass represents time which has not yet passed and, as such, is a potential future indicator of the passage of time, soon to become the past. The image is powerful in its own right as well as being reminiscent of Gerard Manley Hopkins (1844–89), who also used an hourglass in the famous fourth stanza in *The Wreck of the Deutschland* to signify mortality: 'I am soft sift / in an hourglass – at the wall / Fast, but mined with a motion'. Another major poet being alluded to in this section of the poem is T. S. Eliot. In the opening of *Four Quartets* he writes:

> Time present and time past
> Are both perhaps present in time future
> And time future contained in time past.
> If all time is eternally present
> All time is unredeemable.
> What might have been is an abstraction
> Remaining a perpetual possibility
> Only in a world of speculation.
> What might have been and what has been
> Point to one end, which is always present.

The shifts in tenses are important to register in 'Pluto' beside T. S. Eliot's. The past becomes the present in 'I cry out now in my bath, / shocked and bereaved again' (lines 14–15). Memory can be a wonderful and instant means of reliving happy times but, of course, it is not selective enough to obliterate painful experiences like bereavement. He is unable to redeem his childhood, and his past experience of bereavement determined his future, which has become his present. We are left pondering a man who may have had 'perpetual possibility' but it remains just that in a realm that can only be considered speculative. These ideas are returned to repeatedly in *Mean Time*.

When the man says that he is beside himself there is a real sense in which he is actually beside himself by being transformed through

CHECK THE NET

A comprehensive web site devoted to Gerard Manley Hopkins can be found at **http:// www.dundee.ac. uk/english/ hopkins.htm**

CHECK THE BOOK

For a commentary on T. S. Eliot's *Four Quartets*, see Steve Ellis's *The English Eliot: Design, Language and Landscape in 'Four Quartets'* (1991).

memory and olfactory sense into a boy again. The smell of tangerine soap transports the old man back to his boyhood. This particular **image** is reminiscent of Edward Thomas's (1878–1917) poem 'Digging', that begins with the lines: 'To-day I think / Only with scents'. On a more obvious level, though, he is simply articulating an intense feeling of happiness. To be beside oneself is to be experiencing an extremity of emotion.

Duffy invokes another poem, 'Soap Suds' by Louis MacNeice (1907–63). This presents a man washing his hands and being reminded, by the smell of the particular soap brand, of doing the same thing 'in the big / House he visited when he was eight'. The poem closes by musing that there are 'hands / Under the running tap that are not the hands of a child'. We might align the image of the running tap with the trickling sand in the hourglass: both emphasise the irrevocable passage of time. Louis MacNeice belonged to a group that included W. H. Auden and C. Day Lewis. Their verse eschewed deliberately 'poetic' language, embraced the topical and was concerned with social issues. It was the 'new poetry' of the 1930s. The link to be made with Duffy is that she had MacNeice playing as a sort of background music in her head at times and she is very much a poet whose work is considered new. Also, the wistful **tone** of the man presented in 'Pluto' is connected with what he perceives as a less complicated, sympathetic Britain of the 1930s. The influential Bloodaxe anthology *The New Poetry* (1993), edited by Michael Hulse, David Kennedy and David Morley, clearly revisits and attempts to redefine the poetic landscape of Britain. If we remember the preoccupation with time in *Mean Time* it is not difficult to see that even 'Pluto' itself is given part of its context by others.

CHECK THE BOOK
If you wish to find out more about the lives and work of writers mentioned in these Notes, *The Oxford Companion to English Literature*, edited by Margaret Drabble, is a good place to begin.

TEXT 3 – ANNE HATHAWAY (*THE WORLD'S WIFE*)

'Item I gyve unto my wief my second best bed ...'
(from Shakespeare's will)

The bed we loved in was a spinning world
of forests, castles, torchlight, cliff-tops, seas
where he would dive for pearls. My lover's words
were shooting stars which fell to earth as kisses

on these lips; my body now a softer rhyme   5
to his, now echo, assonance; his touch
a verb dancing in the centre of a noun.
Some nights I dreamed he'd written me, the bed
a page beneath his writer's hands. Romance
and drama played by touch, by scent, by taste.   10
In the other bed, the best, our guests dozed on,
dribbling their prose. My living laughing love –
I hold him in the casket of my widow's head
As he held me upon that next best bed.

This poem from *The World's Wife*, written in the voice of
Shakespeare's widow, is immediately accessible because of its
familiar **tone** and the manner in which Anne Hathaway enthuses
about her dead husband. Despite its apparent simplicity, Carol Ann
Duffy uses a rich complexity of ideas relating to language,
relationships and Shakespeare's work. She has chosen to adopt
the sonnet form and this is particularly appropriate as Shakespeare
himself adapted the form and wrote one hundred and fifty-four of
his own sonnets.

The standard sonnet form was known as the Petrarchan, Italian or
regular sonnet, with a rhyme scheme *abba abba cde cde*, but it was
modified thus by Shakespeare: *abab acdc defef gg*. The **volta** is
delayed in his sonnets until the final rhyming **couplet**, although
there is often a discernible change in direction at around line 8, the
traditional position of the volta. Carol Ann Duffy's rhyme scheme
is looser than those already mentioned and employs **half-rhyme**,
something in keeping with the 'softer rhyme' mentioned at the
end of line 5 of this poem. The rhyming couplet conforms to the
Shakespearean model but it does not introduce a new rhyme.
By recalling 'bed' in line 8, the **persona**'s preoccupation with her
physical relationship is brought to the reader's attention.

CONTEXT

The poets Thomas
Wyatt (1503–42)
and Henry
Howard, Earl of
Surrey (1517–47)
were credited with
introducing the
sonnet to England.

It is fitting that Anne Hathaway writes in the form that her husband
so famously used. This in itself is an act of homage and, possibly,
a means of keeping him alive. Shakespeare's famous sonnet 18,
beginning 'Shall I compare thee to a summer's day?' and ending
with 'So long lives this, and this gives life to thee', voices the

commonly held view that humans might die but a work of art can last for ever, effectively immortalising its subject.

Shakespeare, the arch **metaphor**-user and coiner of words, is written about in metaphorical terms even in the first line. The idea of a bed being a 'spinning world' is striking and starts the poem off at a giddying pace. Duffy neatly presents the bed as a microcosmic centre of an imaginative, expansive universe 'of forests, castles, torchlight, cliff-tops, seas' suggesting, at the very least, the plays *As You Like It, Macbeth, Hamlet* and *The Tempest*. The **image** of Shakespeare diving in bed suggests oral sex with Anne Hathaway, as well as reminding us that he was the man who wrote Ariel's song in *The Tempest*.

It is significant that Anne Hathaway describes her husband as a 'lover' (line 3), suggesting that their physical relationship was vital and exciting. This is given further emphasis by the words 'spinning', 'shooting', 'dancing' and 'laughing'. The vitality of their sexual union fits in well with the sort of people we might expect Anne and her husband to be.

Duffy begins with a quotation from Shakespeare's will as an epigraph to the poem. Some commentators, and not only feminists, have taken the statement to be something of a slight on Anne Hathaway. To be left a 'second best bed' is not generally felt to have been complimentary. We might have expected, then, that Anne Hathaway would be given the opportunity to have her revenge. Although other poems in *The World's Wife* do present women as being unhappy with their lot, Anne Hathaway's version of events reveals that she was very much in love with her husband. Theirs was a marriage of equality. He left her his second best bed because it was the one in which they had enacted in a very real sense the drama of their relationship. No children are mentioned by Anne; she concentrates purely on the physical act and not its consequences.

In keeping with the expression of a separate identity, Anne Hathaway is presented as someone who is able to use words in an impressively poetic way. In this sense her personality rhymes with

> **CONTEXT**
>
> *As You Like It* is set in the Forest of Arden, close to Stratford-upon-Avon; *Macbeth* and *Hamlet* are partly set in castles; and *The Tempest* involves a sea voyage.

> **CONTEXT**
>
> An epigraph is a quotation or fragment that writers place at the beginning of poems, novels or chapters as a clue or hint, often somewhat indirect or obscure, towards their meaning.

her husband's. She refers to her body being a 'softer rhyme' to Shakespeare. Here, Duffy is subtly relating the poetic techniques of **masculine rhyme** and **feminine rhyme** to the actual lives of two people who could hardly be separated from art: 'kisses' at the end of line 4 is a feminine ending; 'touch' is a masculine one. This explicit use of linguistic and poetic terms draws attention to the self-conscious **artifice** of the persona's utterance, as well as the poet's.

Hathaway states that her lover's words 'echo' as 'assonance' in her head. The words 'on', 'body', 'softer', 'to', 'echo', 'assonance', 'touch' and 'noun' are all linked by **assonance**; the 'o' sound does indeed echo through the lines as a softer rhyme. The description of Shakespeare's touch as 'a verb dancing in the centre of a noun' creates a vital impression of joyous action. It is sexually suggestive in that his hands could be 'dancing' in the 'centre' of his wife. The line also alerts us to one of Shakespeare's most famous means of energising language; he would often turn nouns into verbs. For example, in *The Winter's Tale* Perdita says, 'I'll *queen* it no inch further' (IV.4.451, my italics). In a practically poetic sense, then, Shakespeare was able to find verbs in the centre of nouns. As is sometimes the case in Shakespeare's sonnets, there is a perceptible progression in this sonnet with 'Some nights' (line 8), but the volta actually occurs after line 12 at the rhyming couplet, providing the clinching idea and sense of **closure**. This rhyme is, incidentally, masculine so we are aware of a female voice giving her husband something of a ghostly, lasting presence in its use. The metaphors in lines 8–9, 'I dreamed he'd written me, the bed / a page beneath his writer's hands', are consistent with Shakespeare's occupation but they also make a forceful statement about the imaginative power of his wife. She desires him so much that she would like to have been one of his dramatic creations. The bed as site of dramatic action is there as a blank for her husband's imagination to be unleashed upon. Visually, sheets could easily be thought of as paper in this context. The blurring of the distinction between life and art is again inherent in this section of the poem. The subsequent 'Romance / and drama played by touch, by scent, by taste' is heavily erotic, concentrating on sensory exploration and not language itself. Lines 8–10 use theatrical imagery to powerful effect in presenting

> **CONTEXT**
>
> Shakespeare delayed the volta in his sonnets until the twelfth line, but there is often a discernible shift of ideas after the second **quatrain**, the point at which a Petrarchan sonnet displays a more noticeable turn.

a scene of lovemaking. The word 'drama' makes reference to plays in general as well as to love, while 'Romance', one of the categories into which some of Shakespeare's plays are placed, also reminds us that this relationship is not stale.

Anne relishes remembering that the 'guests dozed on' while she and William made love. The derogatory 'dribbling their prose' (line 12) is contrasted sharply with 'My living laughing love'. The lilting **alliteration** and the **cadence** of the verse at this point convey extreme happiness and affection. This contrasts with the 'd', 'b' and 'p' sounds in 'dozed', 'dribbling' and 'prose'. The impression created is that the guests live an inferior life of prose. Shakespeare often gave low-status characters prose to speak. The dash preceding the conclusion of the poem acts as something of a dramatic gesture and separates the descriptions of Shakespeare alive with Anne's acknowledgement that he can only live on in her imagination now that he is dead. The fact that she describes her head as a 'casket', a strongbox for keeping jewels and other precious items, indicates the deep love and affection she had for her husband. The **consonance** on 'hold' and 'held' recalls that the lovers rhymed with each other when alive, while the tense change poignantly signals the irrevocable change brought about by her husband's death. The final, clinching rhyme of 'head' and 'bed' indicates that Anne Hathaway is able to keep love alive in her memory and imagination. We are left with Anne Hathaway cherishing the memory of being with her husband in 'that next best bed'. Their true intimacy is made clear here as only she would have been able to interpret correctly Shakespeare's intention when he wrote the famous bequest in his will. His will, in every sense, is hers.

This sonnet, then, is a poem about a poet by a poet, with the intermediary being the subject's surviving partner. Carol Ann Duffy is using this thrown voice as a means of celebrating the subject, Shakespeare.

CHECK THE BOOK

Shakespeare's **sonnets** are published in many editions but among the most authoritative is the Arden edition of 1997, edited by Katherine Duncan-Jones.

CRITICAL APPROACHES

THEMES

Carol Ann Duffy's concerns are numerous and the following comments under thematic headings are, to an extent, artificial, since it is impossible, for example, to separate memory and childhood.

CHILDHOOD

Childhood memory and the experience of it in Carol Ann Duffy's poems are significant but not confined just to her own life. In 'Lizzie, Six' (*Standing Female Nude*) she addresses the issue of child abuse. The words of the child are responded to by an adult whose voice is threatening and concerned only with meting out physical punishment. The short lines of the poem's five **quatrains** are reminiscent of William Blake (1757–1827), whose *Songs of Innocence* (1789) and *Songs of Experience* (1794) explore, among other things, the threat posed by adults to children. The child's open answers to the adult's questions are met with sinister repetition of 'moon', 'fields', 'love', 'wood' and 'dark'. The invasion of childhood innocence by the world of adult experience is also considered in poems such as 'Originally' (*The Other Country*), where 'All childhood is an emigration' (line 9). The reality of moving house leads to initial anxiety about being different, and the rapid process known to linguists as 'accommodation' leaves the child adapting her speech to fit in 'in the classroom sounding just like the rest' (line 21). 'In Mrs Tilscher's Class' in the same collection, the primary-school classroom is 'better than home' (line 9) and 'glowed like a sweet shop' (line 10). The 'emigration' towards adulthood is symbolically presented in the metamorphosis of the tadpoles into frogs and the reality of human sexuality is a lesson learnt in the playground from a 'rough boy', leaving the child to stare 'appalled' at her parents. The rite of passage from childhood to pre-adolescence is signalled in 'You ran through the gates, impatient to be grown, / as the sky split open into a thunderstorm' (lines 29–30). The fact that the child 'ran' emphasises how quickly experience is gained and reminds the reader that part of this adult world includes

www. CHECK THE NET

The comprehensive and informative Blake archive is at **http://www. blakearchive.org**

people like 'Brady and Hindley' (line 11) and the parents in
'We Remember Your Childhood Well'. 'Stafford Afternoons' from
Mean Time was occasioned by the memory of being exposed to by
a man in a park. Despite knowing 'it was dangerous' (line 13), the
part of every child that is tempted to ignore parental warnings led
Duffy to run the gauntlet of the wood where 'the trees / drew sly
faces from light and shade' (lines 13–14). The 'living, purple root
in his hand' (line 19) presents the man who utters 'hoarse, frightful
endearments' (line 21) as an invader of innocence. The child's
natural curiosity can have calamitous results.

The influence of Carol Ann Duffy's Catholic upbringing finds
expression in several poems, either as an object of attack or a source
of **imagery**. In 'Ash Wednesday 1984' (*Standing Female Nude*) the
'Dead language' (line 4) of the Church does not simply refer to
Latin since, as far as she is concerned, it is life-threatening. The
superstitious indoctrination of children taught to see their souls
as 'a vest / spattered with wee black marks' (lines 17–18) is
psychologically damaging, and being 'leathered up the road to
Church' (line 12) underlines the absurdity of such coercion in
the context of what should be a sympathetic experience. 'Words
of Absolution' from the same collection challenges the traditions
of catechism, the doctrines of purgatory and original sin. 'Confession'
is one of a number of poems in *Mean Time* that concentrates
particularly on autobiographical childhood experience. Duffy
rejects what she sees as a male-dominated and stifling religion in
which 'your guardian angel / works your conscience like a glove-
puppet' (lines 2–3).

Joyful aspects of childhood are also explored. 'An Afternoon with
Rhiannon' (*The Other Country*) presents a little girl whose 'small
child's daylight / is a safer place than a poet's slow, appalling, ticking
night' (lines 11–12) and who speaks 'in a voice so new it shines'
(line 13). Pristine, unpolluted innocence is celebrated as a source of
consolation for the fearful poet whose **sonnet** contrasts Rhiannon's
reaction to 'the Building / Larkin feared' – '*I like / buildings!*' –
with her own, '*He was right*'. The separate countries of the adult
and child are neatly suggested in 'The older people look, the shy
town smiles' (line 14), and the reader identifies with the uninhibited

**CHECK
THE BOOK**

For a discussion of
Duffy's writing for a
younger audience,
see Eva Müller-
Zettelmann's essay
'"Skeleton, Moon,
Poet": Carol Ann
Duffy's postmodern
poetry for children'
in *The Poetry of
Carol Ann Duffy:
'Choosing Tough
Words'*, edited by
Angelica Michelis
and Antony
Rowland, pp.
186–201 (2003).

enthusiasm of the child as well as the implied desire of the adults to return to such a state.

MEMORY

Carol Ann Duffy's preoccupation with memory, and its power to both uplift and destroy, is evident in all her collections. Its connection with childhood has been outlined above but it also functions in other ways. As a means of reliving the past it is a vital human capacity. 'In Your Mind' (*The Other Country*) and 'Pluto' (*Mean Time*) are potent explorations of the effects of memory, which can be both personal and collective, a duality that Duffy is not slow to exploit. For example, 'Prayer', the sonnet that concludes *Mean Time*, makes 'the minims sung by a tree' (line 4), 'the distant Latin chanting of a train' (line 8), 'Grade One piano scales' (line 9) and someone who 'calls / a child's name as though they named their loss' (line 12) evoke a past with which the reader can identify. In many respects it is her adroitness in making particular memories universally accessible that contributes to Duffy's popular appeal. As Sean O'Brien said, 'So often with Duffy does the reader say, "Yes, that's it exactly"'.

CHECK THE BOOK

Sean O'Brien's *The Deregulated Muse: Essay on Contemporary British and Irish Poetry* (1998) offers an excellent commentary on Duffy and many other contemporary poets.

Other poems deal with intimate recollection while addressing elements of a national memory or consciousness. 'Père Lachaise' (*The Other Country*) recalls being in the famous Paris cemetery with a friend, but it is also an act of homage to great dead writers, painters and musicians. 'Dream of a Lost Friend' (*The Other Country*) and 'Café Royal' (*Mean Time*) concentrate on commemorating the dead in a way that mixes the experience of personal loss with the issue of Aids.

Of course, memory can be real or imagined. Autobiographical pieces such as 'Originally' need to be set against the memories of personae in 'Havisham', 'Pluto' (*Mean Time*) or 'Anne Hathaway' (*The World's Wife*). Miss Havisham, the woman jilted at the altar, is doomed to relive the memory of this experience, becoming physically atrophied, psychologically damaged and eternally vengeful. She utters 'Puce curses' (line 9), haunted by 'the lost body' (line 10) of the man she never married, leaving her desiring 'a male corpse for a long slow honeymoon' (line 15). In contrast, memory functions as a source of mental balm for the persona in 'Pluto' and he craves the optimistic, uncomplicated past of the time before his parents died and he was placed in a home. The present is a bleak place as he contemplates 'what it was like' (line 23) to be young, his childhood as 'unreachable' (line 22) as the planet Pluto. Anne Hathaway's memories are a kaleidoscopic mixture of impressions of the world's most revered poet and she preserves this in a sonnet, the most appropriate tribute to her 'living laughing love' (line 12). 'Pluto' and 'Anne Hathaway' are discussed in **Extended commentaries**.

Love, relationships and sexuality

The nature of love and relationships is presented in a multifaceted manner. Love is viewed from a variety of perspectives and this is partly made possible by Duffy's ubiquitous use of the **dramatic monologue**. This is not, of course, to ignore the large number of poems that are **lyrics** about love. The various relationships to be found within families are explored, as are those between friends and lovers. The issue of sexuality is approached from both a purely gender based point of view and one that addresses physical relationships. These relationships explore heterosexual and homosexual partnerships in a way that echoes D. H. Lawrence's concern with what he regarded as the otherness of lovers. He was primarily concerned with heterosexual relationships, whereas Duffy explores the 'other country' of lesbianism. Linda France, in her introduction to *Sixty Women Poets* (p. 17), remarks:

> More than ever before the erotic is available to women as theme or metaphor ... This is part of a well-documented female tradition traced back to Sappho and flourishing, despite centuries of oppression, in the works of poets like Aphra Behn, Christina Rossetti and Edna St Vincent Millay.

Such detail should not be lightly passed over. Sappho, the first known European poet, had male as well as female lovers and in view of this is legitimated as a woman who can speak from having had experience of both sexes. 'Girlfriends' and 'Two Small Poems of Desire' (*The Other Country*) present lovers in a highly erotic, sensually charged manner. Carol Ann Duffy's choice of the **sonnet**

CONTEXT

In the ancient world, Sappho was known as 'the Tenth Muse'.

CHECK THE BOOK

For a detailed and illuminating discussion of Englishness and otherness, read Angelica Michelis's essay '"Me not know what these people mean": gender and national identity in Carol Ann Duffy's poetry' in *The Poetry of Carol Ann Duffy: 'Choosing Tough Words'*, edited by Angelica Michelis and Antony Rowland, pp. 77–98 (2003).

form for 'Girlfriends' is appropriate to a love lyric. Her frank presentation of orgasmic sounds in 'Two Small Poems of Desire' communicates a sense of the way the inarticulate sounds of the lover, 'an animal learning vowels' (line 3), actually articulate what she is experiencing at a visceral, extra-linguistic level. Male homosexuality is explored in 'Café Royal' (*Mean Time*), commemorating Oscar Wilde and the consequences of Aids for people like him in a late twentieth-century setting. A brutal, homicidal, heterosexual man is presented in 'Psychopath' (*Selling Manhattan*).

The intensity of love and passion felt for a lover is also memorably recorded in 'Words, Wide Night' (*The Other Country*) in which feeling, as in 'Girlfriends', is beyond language: 'For I am in love with you and this / is what it is like or what it is like in words' (lines 9–10). In 'First Love' (*Mean Time*) Carol Ann Duffy presents the experience named by its title in terms of a memory cherished for life 'as close to my lips as lipstick' (line 2) and 'an old film played at a slow speed' (line 8). There may be a 'changing sky' (line 9) but the love will remain in the memory.

The destructive potentials of love are explored in 'Eley's Bullet' (*The Other Country*) whose protagonist 'wished to God / he'd never loved' (stanza 9) as he decides whether or not to 'open his mouth / for a gun with his name on its bullet to roar / in his brains' (stanza 9). The breakdown of relationships is explored in 'Adultery' (*Mean Time*), characterised by a powerful portrait of the adulterer 'slim with deceit' (line 10) sending flowers that are 'dumb and explicit on nobody's birthday' (line 36). 'Disgrace' (*Mean Time*) reads like an elegy for a broken relationship. Communication has ceased between the lovers, their 'words changed. Dead flies in a web' (line 5). All three of these poems employ a regular stanzaic structure reflecting the inescapable temporal progression of time. 'Valentine' (*Mean Time*) employs an extended **metaphor** in a manner reminiscent of the **metaphysical poets'** use of the **conceit** to explore the dangerous dimension of committing oneself to a long-term relationship. An onion, the unusual valentine offered as a gift to the lover, may be 'a moon wrapped in brown paper' (line 3) but 'Its scent will cling to your fingers, / cling to your knife' (lines 22–3).

Duffy's love poems for her mother are memorable for their clear communication of love without sentimentality. 'The Way My Mother Speaks' (*The Other Country*) celebrates mothers as repositories of culture and a source of strength. 'Before You Were Mine' (*Mean Time*) reminds us that mothers are people in their own right and had very different lives before hearing the 'loud, possessive yell' (line 11) of children.

LANGUAGE

Duffy's use of language is much noted for its resistance of the studiously poetic. As Wordsworth attempted to, she succeeds in writing in an immediately recognisable and accessible idiom. Her **diction** very much reflects the fact that she is able to articulate what many ordinary people feel. This is not to suggest, however, that her poems are simple. She uses straightforward language in complex ways.

Her **lyrics** articulate sentiment in a memorable way but are never sentimental. They have the authentic sound of the modern but are never in danger of being ephemeral. W. B. Yeats said that poetry should be concerned with 'telegrams and anger', an acknowledgement that the poet cannot be in lyrical repose or pastoral retreat but has to address the reality of the here and now. Carol Ann Duffy's own attraction to what Seamus Heaney calls the 'come hither of the lyric' is quite clear, but she tempers this with an acute awareness of real, contemporary situations. Her affinity with the French **surrealists** and the Liverpool Poets results in her giving space to the metropolitan, often finding lyric moments in it. In words that could easily describe Duffy's approach Yeats also said:

> I tried to make the language of poetry coincide with that of passionate, normal speech. I wanted to write in whatever language comes most naturally when we soliloquise, as I do all day long, upon the events of our own lives or of any life where we can see ourselves for the moment.
>
> (*Essays and Introductions*, p. 521)

 CHECK THE NET
An excerpt from Gerard Durozoi's book about André Breton and the Surrealist Manifesto may be found at **http://www. fathom.com/ feature/122621**

LANGUAGE continued

CHECK THE BOOK

See my '"What it is like in words": translation, reflection and refraction in the poetry of Carol Ann Duffy' in *The Poetry of Carol Ann Duffy: 'Choosing Tough Words'*, edited by Angelica Michelis and Antony Rowland, pp. 169–85 (2003), for a discussion of some of Duffy's linguistic concerns.

Language itself is explored by Duffy as a system of communication, signification and, sometimes, obfuscation. 'Nostalgia' (*Mean Time*) equates a physical journey with an exploration of the **etymology** of that word. 'Words, Wide Night' (*The Other Country*) reflects upon the inability of words to express what is felt, thought or imagined. Words are, as Heraclitus said, 'fallible things', but are also, as Terry Eagleton points out, 'the shared counters of experience'. Language becomes a system that refracts meaning rather than one that truly reflects what the user intends. Duffy articulates this tension very clearly in this thought-provoking 'impossible song of desire' (line 6).

The philosophy of language was a feature of Carol Ann Duffy's undergraduate study at Liverpool University and she was particularly interested in Ludwig Wittgenstein (1889–1951), whose *Tractatus* (1922) deals with the limitations and possibilities of language (see **Extended Commentaries: Text 1**). Duffy repeatedly questions and tests its ability to articulate what is required of it. 'Words, Wide Night' is a good example of this interrogation of language.

The issue of translation is another facet of her interest in language, as is made clear in 'Translating the English, 1989' (*The Other Country*). Duffy seizes on the **cliché** of the English invention of a foreigner talking of 'the English' instead of 'English' and uses the term against such people as they are the ones who have become **metaphorically** 'translated' by the emergence of what she saw as a xenophobic, individualistic, nationalistic society. 'The Dolphins' (*Standing Female Nude*) tries to find a language to give these animals a voice in much the same way as Les Murray presents a range of creatures in *Translations from the Natural World* (1992). The dolphin says of its companion, 'The other's movement / forms my thoughts' (lines 4–5). It articulates its gradual acclimatisation to the aquarium in which it finds itself in terms of translation: 'After travelling such space for days we began / to translate' (lines 10–11). The dolphins' language is form and shape. 'Translation' (*Selling Manhattan*) is a **sonnet** set in a gritty bar telling the story of a seduction, but as it progresses words become translated into the actions of love. The sound of the one-armed bandit 'cranking

Bugger bugger bugger' (line 7) suggests the rhythm of sex referred to in line 11. 'River' (*The Other Country*) uses words as a means of showing the way they reflect, and are rooted in, other countries or cultures. However, 'Water crosses the border, / translates itself' (lines 3–4) in a manner that transcends such restriction, unlike the baby in 'Brothers' (*Mean Time*) whose pre-linguistic, pre-reflective self is 'like a new sound flailing for a shape' (line 8).

The way a society uses language is an index of its attitudes and identity. This is made clear in poems from all six of Duffy's collections. 'Standing Female Nude' (*Standing Female Nude*) examines the power transactions between men and women. The artist 'possesses' (line 18) his model on canvas but she asserts herself through economic means, 'I say / Twelve francs' (lines 27–8) and the final, triumphant dismissal of his work: 'It does not look like me' (line 28). The plethora of insulting names that Mrs Quasimodo (*The World's Wife*) lists, such as '*pig*', '*stupid cow*', '*fucking buffalo*', indicates how men have a seemingly inexhaustible supply of such terms for women. They, like the Quasimodo in the poem, cannot accept someone who does not live up to the ideal of a svelte gypsy girl or similar male-manufactured icon.

POLITICS

Carol Ann Duffy deals with a number of political events and issues in her poems (see **Detailed commentaries** and **Historical and political background**). Linked to this is the matter of sexual politics, the relative positions of men and women in society. This facet of political reality may be connected with Marxism. The relationship between Marxism and feminism is significant since both view society as being driven by power structures that tend to polarise it. Duffy found her socialist sympathies at odds with a monetarist, capitalist Tory government.

Several of her poems deal with this conflict explicitly while in others the political commentary is still present, however implicit. Having lived through the 1960s and 1970s, many people of left-wing liberal sympathies found Margaret Thatcher's government autocratic and unsympathetic to the least fortunate in society. Her 'monetarism' became known for its contention that wealth could 'trickle down'

CHECK THE BOOK

For comment on politics in Duffy's poetry, see the introduction to *The Poetry of Carol Ann Duffy: 'Choosing Tough Words'*, edited by Angelica Michelis and Antony Rowland, pp. 18–20 (2003).

CONTEXT

Marxist criticism considers literature in relation to its capacity to reflect the struggle between the classes, and the economic conditions which, according to Karl Marx (1818–83) and Friedrich Engels (1820–95), lie at the basis of humankind's intellectual and social evolution.

from the 'top' of society to the 'bottom'. Radical feminism was radically disappointed in a female prime minister who seemed to display all the worst traits of men. In the landmark Bloodaxe anthology, *Sixty Women Poets* (1993), its editor Linda France observed (p. 17):

> Feminism did not die under the rule of Britain's first woman Prime Minister. But what should have been a blessing turned out to be a curse; and not only for women.

Margaret Thatcher became the darling of the right-wing press, and *The Sun* newspaper famously claimed the credit for her re-election with the headline 'It Was the Sun Wot Won It'. Another notorious headline in *The Sun* was 'Gotcha!', its response to the sinking of the Argentinian ship the *General Belgrano*. It is precisely this sort of journalism that is attacked in 'Poet for Our Times' (*The Other Country*). The intoxicated journalist who speaks in the poem seems to encapsulate for Duffy the low cultural ebb reached by a society with no more ambition for its young than that they be fed on a diet of tabloid headlines. The man in question has a 'dream' (line 25) that 'kids will know my headlines off by heart' (line 26). The high circulation of such newspapers is a further source of dismay for Duffy as they also peddle prurient, scandalous stories about people, fuelling racism and xenophobia as illustrated by such couplets as: 'IMMIGRANTS FLOOD IN CLAIMS HEATHROW WATCHER. / GREEN PARTY WOMAN IS A NIGHTCLUB TART' (lines 27–8). Duffy's use of upper-case letters **satirises** the raucous technique of tabloids that 'just bang the words down like they're screaming *Fire!*' (line 4).

The very fact of being a poet in Britain in the 1980s and 1990s was, in Duffy's view, to be politicised. Being a woman poet in the prevailing climate made this even more acutely felt. Politicians are fond of telling people not to interfere in politics while pursuing courses of action that profoundly influence every citizen's life. In a direct challenge to the then prime minister, John Major (whose full surname is Major-Ball), Duffy tells him in 'Like Earning a Living' (*Mean Time*):

Somewhere in England, Major-Balls,
the long afternoon empties of air, meaning, energy, point.
Kin-L. There just aren't the words for it. (lines 15–17)

This paints a bleak picture of England as a stultifying place lacking
in opportunity. The last line quoted above is not just the voice of
an unimaginative, disaffected youth but that of an angry poet who
felt that the gap between those with prospects and those with
none progressively increased with each successive Conservative
government.

This sort of issue, and others under the Thatcher administration,
such as Care in the Community, the Dangerous Dogs Act, and
salmonella in eggs, are dealt with in 'Translating the English, 1989'
(*The Other Country*). Many people in Britain were beginning
to despair at the thought of a Conservative victory in the 1997
general election. Carol Ann Duffy's poem 'The Act of Imagination'
(*The Other Country*) puts 'Ten More Years' at the top of a list of
things that '*may be / prosecuted for appalling the Imagination*'.
Margaret Thatcher spoke of wanting to remain in power for another
ten years at one of her party conferences. Carol Ann Duffy saw this
as a terrible prospect. The use of the capital letter in '*Imagination*'
shows that she feels it needs to be given precedence in a country
that seemed to be putting profit before principle. There is a clear
pun on the word '*Act*' since it refers to both the imaginative pursuit
by a poet of the art and also an act of parliament. Another poem,
'The Literature Act' (*The Other Country*), uses the same punning
idea to indict the sort of atavistic male that 'yob culture' in the
1980s seemed to condone.

The euphoria and optimism that was felt by many following the
Labour Party's landslide victory in the 1997 general election left its
sympathisers expecting a lot of change. The prosecution of a second
war in the Gulf and Britain's seeming inability to say no to America
leaves quite a proportion of natural Labour supporters uneasy.
Latterly, Duffy has found these same sympathies at odds with the
incumbent Labour administration which, at the time of writing,
faces a general election in 2005.

**CHECK
THE BOOK**
For a discussion of
'Poet for Our Times'
and 'Translating the
English, 1989', see
Neil Roberts's essay
'Duffy, Eliot and
impersonality'
in *The Poetry of
Carol Ann Duffy:
'Choosing Tough
Words'*, edited by
Angelica Michelis
and Antony
Rowland, pp. 39–40
(2003).

TIME

The relationship between individuals and time is inescapable. Carol Ann Duffy places this at the centre of her fourth collection, *Mean Time*, but as a theme, time features in earlier collections too. Time can seem to be malevolent ('The clocks slid back an hour / and stole light from my life', 'Mean Time', lines 1–2), all-powerful ('but time owns us', 'Brothers', line 15) or an inexorable, depressing reminder of mortality ('An hourglass weeping the future into the past', 'Pluto', line 12). Its link with memory is obvious but it is worth remembering that the effects of time and its seemingly elastic qualities fascinate Duffy. 'In Your Mind' (*The Other Country*), for example, shows how years can be remembered in a moment.

POETIC FORM

www. CHECK THE NET
For more information about W. B. Yeats, together with online versions of his work, go to **http://www.online-literature.com**

Carol Ann Duffy inherits a rich heritage from traditional British and European poetry, as well as the **avant-garde** movement of the early decades of the twentieth century. She employs a wide variety of forms that include *vers libre* or **free verse**; the **sonnet**; and, of course, the **dramatic monologue**. Her adept adoption of traditional forms confirms her affinity with W. H. Auden. Unlike Yeats she does not feel uncomfortable with free verse but her determination to pace the known paths of the **quatrain** align her with him.

THE DRAMATIC MONOLOGUE

Carol Ann Duffy's use of the dramatic monologue aligns her with Robert Browning, whose *Dramatis Personae*, published in 1864, includes such famous poems as 'Fra Lippo Lippi' and 'My Last Duchess'. Browning said he tried to write 'poetry always dramatic in principle, and so many utterances of so many imaginary persons, not mine'. He had written unsuccessfully for the theatre and his monologues:

> presented some character thinking aloud in a moment of stress or at some point of crisis: confiding to the reader, in his or her individual idiom, the conflicts of thought and emotion involved in this particular predicament.
>
> (Margaret Willy, *Browning's Men and Women*, 1968, p. 7)

In Duffy's poetry this writing technique is a unifying principle in a diversity of voices ranging from the bewildered immigrant child in 'Comprehensive' (*Standing Female Nude*) to the jilted Miss Havisham (*Mean Time*) and the confident, intellectually independent Frau Freud (*The World's Wife*). Duffy's publication of the pamphlet *Thrown Voices* in 1986 drew attention through its title to her affinity with the dramatic monologue. What is so impressive about these monologues is her ability to tune into the frequency of transmission of the voice she chooses to articulate.

Clumsily handled, the dramatic monologue can seem unconvincing and artificial but Duffy always gives the impression of spontaneity. This is distinct from the archly deliberate manner in which she sometimes draws attention to the medium she has chosen to employ. This is amply illustrated in 'The Dummy' (*Selling Manhattan*), where the mannequin makes us aware that the ventriloquist's hand is up its back: 'You can do getter than that, can't you?' This, added to the fact that the poem is a finely crafted sonnet, demonstrates a consummate control over form, voice and technique. This poem also reminds us that Duffy is able to use the sonnet as a vehicle for the monologue as well as the extended free verse of later poems such as '*from* Mrs Tiresias' or 'Mrs Quasimodo' (*The World's Wife*).

Michael Schmidt, in *Lives of the Poets* (1998), says of the satirical aspect of Duffy's dramatic monologues: 'Her Aunt Sallys have nothing in common with Auden's: she gives them a fighting chance' (p. 994). This emphasises her refusal to condemn, but neither does she condone those individuals who resort to violence ('Psychopath', *Selling Manhattan*), theft ('Stealing', *Selling Manhattan*) or escapism ('Liar', *The Other Country*).

All the poems in *The World's Wife* (1999) are dramatic monologues. Deryn Rees-Jones says of them:

> On the one hand the monologues are probably the most overtly feminist of her *oeuvre*; on the other, they are also fantastically removed from reality. As such, they allow Carol Ann Duffy to encode the personal within the characters from myth and

CHECK THE BOOK
Deryn Rees-Jones discusses Duffy's use of the dramatic monologue in the second chapter, 'Masquerades', of her excellent *Carol Ann Duffy*, pp. 17–29 (1999).

history, as well as making feminist statements about the absence
of women from history, or their misrepresentation.

(Carol Ann Duffy, p. 29)

The extensive use of **myth** also reminds us that as attempts to make
sense of the world the poems should be read as just that. This is
emphasised by Duffy's reworking or redefinition of myths. The
power of the human voice has always been at the centre of protest
and the monologues draw attention to the historical fact of male
domination and female suppression. The strength of position from
which Duffy writes in these poems is one that she has been largely
influential in achieving for women's poetry. Realising the
importance of giving women a voice, she remembers crucial figures
in the women's movement. The Kray sisters pay homage to the
suffragettes, Germaine Greer and a host of successful female actors
and singers. In doing this, Duffy presents the liberated women of
the 1960s acknowledging their debt to those who spoke out against
oppression. As a woman writing at the beginning of the twenty-first
century in a country where women have only had the vote since
1928, Duffy makes it clear to men that women do not need marriage
and that the world's wife usually wants a divorce.

 **CHECK
THE NET**
A wealth of
information about
the sonnet may be
found at **http://
www.sonnets.org**

THE SONNET

There can be few modern poets who have put the **sonnet** to such
varied use. Carol Ann Duffy writes a plangent **lyric** in 'Prayer'
(*Mean Time*), a **satire** on parliamentary procedure in 'Weasel
Words' (*The Other Country*), a statement by Myra Hindley ('The
Devil's Wife', *The World's Wife*) and a celebration of the form itself
in 'Anne Hathaway' (*The World's Wife*). There are also sonnets that
are more traditional in having love as their subject. Among these
are 'Saying Something' (*Standing Female Nude*), 'Girlfriends'
(*The Other Country*) and 'Anne Hathaway' (*The World's Wife*).
However, they do not always observe traditional rhyme schemes.
Like Wordsworth's nun, Duffy does not 'fret' within the confines
of the sonnet's 'scanty plot of ground' but finds liberation in its
restrictions. She also uses the form itself to make a particular point.
For example, 'The Literature Act' (*The Other Country*) takes poetic
revenge on the mentality of an emblematic 'yob' who 'spent the
morning demonstrating in the market square / for the benefit of the

gutter press' (lines 3–4). In 'not censoring / the words and pictures in his head' (lines 10–11), his total lack of self-control is thrown into sharp relief by the formal control of the sonnet.

IMAGERY

As a poet widely read in the British and European poetic traditions, there is a fresh diversity in Carol Ann Duffy's use of imagery. Her metaphors can be surreal, abstract or very familiar. One of her most notable gifts is the presentation of abstractions in concrete terms. She clearly has an affinity with the French Symbolists, and with T. S. Eliot and Samuel Beckett, while her connection with the Romantic tradition is evident. William Wordsworth in particular is a confirmatory source in terms of the importance of childhood and memory, while her sensuousness has echoes of the luxuriance of John Keats. Since Duffy's poetic defies what would ultimately be a reductive categorisation, as a feminist poet it is significant that she both acknowledges and draws upon a tradition in poetry that includes several male poets. The influence of the visual arts cannot be ignored, as evidenced by several poems that are directly derived from responses to paintings or artists. In particular, the influence of surrealists should be registered. Among Duffy's favourites are René Magritte and Max Ernst, and their juxtaposition of the ordinary and extraordinary finds expression in her own aesthetic. The trees in 'The Grammar of Light' (*Mean Time*) 'think in birds' (line 12), while in 'Away and See' (*Mean Time*) the instruction is to 'Away and see an ocean suck at a boiled sun' (line 1), and we see 'the flight / of syllables, wingspan stretching a noun' (lines 9–10). 'The Virgin Punishing the Infant' (*Selling Manhattan*) uses Max Ernst's painting as a starting point for a monologue observed by one of the men looking through a window and speaking for a community and its reaction to the Holy Family.

> **CONTEXT**
>
> Romanticism is a term used to describe the philosophical and literary movement dating from 1789, the French Revolution, to about 1830. It stressed the central importance of the imagination, the individual and nature as a source of moral knowledge. Among the best-known English Romantics are Blake, Wordsworth, Coleridge, Southey (first generation Romantics); and Byron, Shelley and Keats (second generation).

PART FOUR

CRITICAL HISTORY

A POET FOR OUR TIMES – THE CRITICAL RECEPTION OF CAROL ANN DUFFY'S WORK

Carol Ann Duffy came to prominence in 1985 with the publication of her first collection, *Standing Female Nude*. Since then, her work has enjoyed increasing critical acclaim. The recipient of several major awards and prizes (see **Carol Ann Duffy's life and work**), she has established a growing reputation. She has been at the forefront of what may be fairly described as an explosion in women's poetry. This has coincided with an unprecedented interest in poetry in general and women's poetry in particular.

The large number of poetry readings and festivals that give people the chance to hear poets reading their work is testament to the fact that poetry has considerable appeal in Britain and beyond. Duffy's readings are among the most popular and she has always been associated with performance. Her involvement with the Liverpool Poets since the 1970s indicates her commitment to the stage as well as the page. This association also aligns her with an approach to poetry that does not seek to retreat into the obscure and the academic. This does not mean, though, that she is not an intellectually challenging poet. Her work is coming under increasing scrutiny as the subject of undergraduate and postgraduate attention. No one has been more energetic in the promotion of poetry in all walks of life. Delighted when Penguin first published its 'Modern Poets' series, she welcomed its commitment to making poetry accessible to a wider public than some of more traditional publishing houses. Her inclusion in *Penguin Modern Poets 2* (1995), a revival of the earlier series, signals her importance as one of the nation's popular poetic voices. She is widely anthologised and is a sought-after editor of anthologies. Her international reputation has been recognised in the form of academic appointments (see **Carol Ann Duffy's life and work**).

CONTEXT

The Liverpool Poets was the name given to a group of three poets, Adrian Henri (1932–2000), Roger McGough (1937–) and Brian Patten (1946–), who utilised the fame of Liverpool as a centre of youth culture during the era of the Beatles to publicise their work by giving it a group identity.

THE LITERATURE ACT – WAYS OF READING

The postmodern climate that is tending to prevail in academic institutions has resulted in an **eclectic** approach to literary criticism. Although there are critics who remain committed to a particular position, many scholars adopt an approach appropriate to the analysis of any given text. This is quite a liberating state of affairs in relation to reading Carol Ann Duffy's works, because it avoids the possibility of their being viewed from a purely feminist perspective. This is not to suggest, though, that a feminist reading is not important, but as Duffy has herself said that she has never deliberately set out to write a single feminist poem, we should be wary of imposing such a gloss on the poems.

A formalist critic would pay close attention to the manner in which the writing draws attention to its own construction. As a linguistic construct it is an artefact. 'The Dummy' (*Selling Manhattan*) is a good example of a poem that lends itself to such an interpretation. The formal organisation of the **sonnet** is often used by Duffy as a counterpoint for the colloquial idiom employed, and this poem is no exception.

A psychoanalytical critic would draw attention to the validity of a Freudian reading. Jane E. Thomas suggests that:

> anyone familiar with Freudian theories of the unconscious might see Duffy's dummy as a metaphor for that dark repository of repressions and socially taboo desires which constantly irrupts into our conscious existence in the form of dreams, fantasies and 'Freudian slips'.
>
> ('"The Intolerable Wrestle with Words": The Poetry of Carol Ann Duffy', *Bête Noire*, 6 (Winter 1998), p. 79)

A male Freudian critic might point out that the repeated motif of the female emasculating the male does suggest the very penis envy that Frau Freud claims is 'pity'. Miss Havisham claims 'I suddenly bite awake' from her erotic dream, Mrs Aesop threatens to cut off the 'little cock that wouldn't crow' and the Kray sisters have clubs

CHECK THE BOOK

Terry Eagleton's *Literary Theory: An Introduction* (1996) is well worth reading as a clear introduction to what is a complex field of study.

CONTEXT

Formalism was a short-lived literary movement in Russia, starting about 1917, which concentrated on form, style and technique in art, excluding other considerations, such as social, political or philosophical aspects.

called 'Ballbreakers' and 'Prickteasers'. Such an argument would be countered by feminists who would point out that it derives from men's deep-seated anxiety about their own sexual identity. They might also suggest that the phenomenon of men's groups such as those organised by the American poet Robert Bly (1926–), which seek to rediscover and reassert their masculinity, attests to the success of women in taking a powerful place in society. Whatever the arguments, it is undeniable that physical, sexual mutilation of women has been a feature of some cultures, drawing attention to the idea that where and when a poem is read can have significant impact.

The Irish woman poet Eavan Boland sees Carol Ann Duffy's achievement as one that challenges and alters power relationships by making women both the subject and object of love poems. John Keats's 'The Eve of St Agnes' (1819) includes the detail of a woman wearing pearls, which are, Boland says, 'erotic objects'. They represent the male conception of women as objects of desire. In comparison, 'Warming Her Pearls' is:

> a bold subversion of the sexualised erotic, a lyric which reassembles the love poem so that it becomes, like the handwriting in the mirror, a menacing reversed message: The speaker is powerless, while the object of her affections has a power which puts her well beyond possession by either desire or expression. The pearls are not the fixed object of Keats's poem. They are the flawed, wounded and ironised object of the traditional poem, but this time held in common between women, rather than perceived as a fixed object, distanced from the speaker.
>
> (*Object Lessons: The Life of the Woman and the Poet in Our Time*, pp. 226–7)

The power transactions between male and female may be absent but there is still the issue of social class acting as a boundary between the women. In this approach we may detect something of the Marxist feminist position which stresses the significance of the patriarchal power structures underpinning society. In fact, some feminists argue that language itself is inscribed with codes that privilege the male, giving it a gender. Peter Schwenger, in *Phallic Critiques: Masculinity and Twentieth-Century Literature* (1984), challenges this position, taking issue with Hélène Cixous's contention that 'language conceals an invincible adversary because it's the language of men and their grammar':

> I distrust all attempts to assign a gender to language. Inevitably these tell us less about language than about the state of mind of those who are assigning a gender to it. If we clearly understand that we are studying the perceivers rather than the language they perceive then there is value in examining these attempts.
>
> (*Phallic Critiques: Masculinity and Twentieth-Century Literature*, p. 19)

Peter Schwenger does acknowledge, though, that there is a distinct language of men but that it 'may be less distinct from women's than is generally assumed' (p. 24). Looked at from another perspective we might say that women's language is less distinct from men's than is generally assumed. Men's language can often change when they are thrown together, often using obscene speech and a lot of **slang**. The use of both these modes in several poems such as 'Mrs Quasimodo', 'Delilah' and 'The Kray Sisters', all from *The World's Wife*, presents women taking over the 'manor' of male language.

Having considered briefly the implications of language and gender, the problems language presents as a system of signification should be considered, especially as this is something that preoccupies Carol Ann Duffy herself. Deryn Rees-Jones argues that Carol Ann Duffy has a 'distrust of language as mediator between idea and object'. And that:

> For Duffy an exploration of the relationship between language and experience always dramatises the gap between signifier and **signified**; between what it about to be said, and what is then said; between the possibility of what might be said, and what can never be said. And this distrust of language leads her to an aesthetic that privileges experience over the telling of the experience ...
>
> (*Carol Ann Duffy*, p. 14)

CHECK THE BOOK

Antony Rowland's essay 'Love and masculinity in the poetry of Carol Ann Duffy' is a thorough study of the presentation of the male, and can be found in *The Poetry of Carol Ann Duffy: 'Choosing Tough Words'*, edited by Angelica Michelis and Antony Rowland, pp. 56–76 (2003).

CONTEXT

Deconstruction, or deconstructive criticism, is a blanket title for certain radical critical theories that revise and develop the tenets of structuralist criticism. Many of the ideas of deconstruction originate in the work of French philosopher Jacques Derrida (1930–), who believes that all notions of the existence of an absolute meaning in language (a 'transcendental signified') are wrong.

The crucial terms 'signifier' and 'signified' in the quotation above refer to the terms used by Swiss linguist Ferdinand de Saussure (1857–1913), who argued that language is a system of **signs** each comprised of a signifier and a signified. Words can only mean, he said, in relation to one another. Further, once the relationship between the signifier and signified has been established, it remains fixed. For example, the signifier 'cat' refers to the signified, a fur-covered four-legged animal. Such a model of language formed the basis of structuralist criticism. If applied to Duffy's poetry this approach suggests that words in themselves have no essential meaning. Duffy does not appear to subscribe to this view but she does, as has been described elsewhere, explore the inadequacy of words in certain circumstances. The post-structuralists, whose primary approach in terms of literary criticism centres on what has come to be known as deconstruction, question the stability of the relationship between the signifier and signified and argue that a text cannot have an essential, guaranteed meaning. A deconstructive critic could, for example, read 'Away and See' (*Mean Time*) as a poem that purports to escape the confines of language but only succeeds in drawing attention to its own reliance upon language as a means of articulating frustration concerning that very reliance.

PART FIVE

BACKGROUND

CAROL ANN DUFFY'S LIFE AND WORK

Carol Ann Duffy was born in Glasgow in 1955. She moved to Stafford at the age of six with her parents and four brothers. She was brought up in a traditional working-class Roman Catholic family and attended St Joseph's Convent and Stafford Girls' High School. Many of her poems reflect a close familiarity with the practices of the Catholicism she rejected.

She always wanted to be a writer and was given a great deal of sympathetic encouragement by her teachers. Some of her very early poems were published while she was at school. Her father was a Labour councillor in Stafford and this undoubtedly gave his daughter an early insight into political matters, something in which she has maintained a clear interest. She studied philosophy at Liverpool University from 1974 to 1977. After graduating, she worked for Granada Television. In the early 1980s she became a freelance writer in London, working as a writer in residence in East End schools. In 1985 she became a full-time writer. As well as poetry she has written plays. *Take My Husband* (1982) and *Cavern of Dreams* (1984) were performed at the Liverpool Playhouse. *Grimm Tales* and *More Grimm Tales*, both written with Tim Supple, have been staged at The Young Vic in London.

Carol Ann Duffy has been the recipient of several important poetry prizes and awards. She won a Scottish Arts Council Book Award for *Standing Female Nude*, a Somerset Maugham Award in 1988 and the Dylan Thomas Award for 1989. *Mean Time* won both the Forward and Whitbread prizes for poetry in 1993. She worked as a writer in residence in London schools between 1982 and 1984. In 1995 a Lannan Literary Award allowed her to teach at Wake Forest University, North Carolina. She is frequently a tutor on Arvon creative writing courses and is committed to promoting poetry in schools and beyond. She currently teaches creative writing to postgraduate students at Manchester Metropolitan University,

> **CONTEXT**
>
> Carol Ann Duffy is Professor of Creative Writing at Manchester Metropolitan University.

where she is Professor of Creative Writing. Her first collection, *Standing Female Nude*, was published to great critical acclaim in 1985. Since then, she has published five other major collections: *Selling Manhattan* (1987), *The Other Country* (1990), *Mean Time* (1993), *The World's Wife* (1999) and *Feminine Gospels* (2002). Penguin published her *Selected Poems* in 1994. Her *New Selected Poems 1984–2004* was published in 2004 by Picador. Duffy's collections appear frequently on examination syllabuses at GCSE and Advanced levels, as well as receiving serious attention at universities. In 1995 Carol Ann Duffy was awarded the OBE in recognition of her services to poetry, the same year in which her daughter, Ella, was born. In 1999 she was made a Fellow of the Royal Society of Literature and published *Meeting Midnight* and *Rumpelstiltskin and Other Grimm Tales* for children. In 2000 Duffy was awarded a five-year fellowship by the National Endowment of Science, Technology and the Arts (NESTA). In 2001 she was awarded a CBE for services to poetry.

> **CONTEXT**
>
> The National Endowment of Science, Technology and the Arts (NESTA) was established in 1998 to support creative potential and innovation in the UK.

HISTORICAL AND POLITICAL BACKGROUND

Although Carol Ann Duffy is very much a living poetic voice, it is important to consider some of the major events that have occurred in her lifetime that have, in one way or another, affected her poetry. The time between 1955 and the present has been a period of extraordinary change both in Britain and worldwide.

Duffy was born ten years after the end of the Second World War into a Britain that was just beginning to emerge from a fairly protracted period of economic depression. The 1950s also saw a large immigrant population arriving in Britain from India and the Caribbean. Many of these people settled in the larger conurbations of London, Birmingham, Manchester and Glasgow. This led simultaneously to the creation of a multicultural, multi-ethnic, cosmopolitan Britain, and the phenomenon of racial intolerance and discrimination. Many argued that the influx of immigrants was an inevitable consequence of British colonialism, while others observed that the need for cheap labour in such areas as public transport was a primary consideration. Racial tensions were to erupt into violent confrontations in Toxteth, Liverpool and Handsworth, Birmingham in the early 1980s.

For some years, at least, Britain seemed to be the land of opportunity for many. This optimistic mood was felt both here and in the United States. The British prime minister, Harold Macmillan, and the American president, John F. Kennedy, met on English soil in 1963. Macmillan was a Tory and Kennedy a Democrat. Both were extremely popular politicians. This led to an even greater feeling of optimism. The economy in Britain boomed and Macmillan famously told Britons: 'You've never had it so good'.

The decade became known as the 'swinging sixties'. The explosion in popular culture that was effectively imported to Britain from America brought with it a radically new way of regarding young people. With the advent of rock and roll, performers such as Bill Haley and the Comets and, most influentially, Elvis Presley, the concept of the teenager was born. British groups like the Liverpool-based Beatles were phenomenally successful worldwide. Changes in attitudes to authority, a growth in drug culture and the development of the contraceptive pill led to what came to be called a 'liberated' generation. Facets of this included 'free love' and 'psychedelia'. Fashions in clothes, music and just about everything else changed radically. This was the age of 'flower power' and festivals such as those on the Isle of Wight in Britain and Woodstock in America.

Not all was associated with 'peace and love' in the 1960s, though. Political events often formed a sinister backdrop on the world stage. The Vietnam War that had started in 1955 was bitterly opposed by many Americans. The Cuban Missile Crisis in 1962 saw Kennedy face down the Russians, who had managed to insinuate forty-two missiles into Cuba. Although it has since become clear that it was probably American ground-force superiority that decided matters rather than a willingness on either side to deploy nuclear weapons, the episode reminded people that the threat of annihilation was very real. The so-called 'Cold War' was at its height during this period.

On 22 November 1963, John Kennedy was assassinated in Dallas, Texas. This event had a profound effect worldwide. It showed that

CHECK THE NET

Search the Internet for more information about the Vietnam War, the Cuban Missile Crisis and the Cold War.

even the most powerful nation on earth, the one that would win the 'space race' on 20 July 1969 by putting man on the moon, was vulnerable. The civil rights activist Martin Luther King was assassinated on 4 April 1968, and Robert Kennedy, brother of the late president, was gunned down on 5 June of the same year.

There was close liaison and traffic of ideas between America and Britain in this period. The so-called 'special relationship' between the two nations exists to this day and proved to be highly significant with regard to such events as the Gulf War in 1990 and the Kosovo crisis of 1999. The second Gulf War in April 2003 ousted Saddam Hussein but, at the time of writing, the continued occupation of Baghdad and the continuing slaughter in Fallujah seem depressingly familiar features of the way American foreign policy has been pursued in the past forty years or so. Iraq, some argue, is America's new Vietnam. It is also, of course, Britain's problem too, since our government stands 'shoulder to shoulder' with the USA in what has become known as 'the global war on terror'.

> **CONTEXT**
>
> Both John Major and Tony Blair are keen advocates of peace in Northern Ireland.

In Britain, the 1960s closed having seen the Moors Murders and, in 1969, the beginning of the modern 'troubles' in Northern Ireland. The Irish problem proved to be a running sore that has yet to be fully healed. The 1970s were noted for economic recession, the 'three-day week' and what came to be regarded as excessive trade union power. A gloomier outlook replaced the optimism of the previous decade. When Margaret Thatcher, the first woman prime minister in history, was elected to power in 1979, many believed that the country's fortunes would improve. Her period in office was characterised by her preference for allowing 'market forces' to shape the economy, in contrast to a more interventionist socialist position.

The quashing of the miners' strike of 1984 proved that the unions were practically impotent. The country went to war with Argentina in 1982 over the Falkland Islands in the South Atlantic because of a dispute over sovereignty. After the war the Tories were returned to power with a huge majority in 1983. Some commentators argued that the jingoistic mood of the nation had contributed greatly to this. The early and mid 1980s saw the economy booming again.

Some people were becoming very rich and a particular group known as 'yuppies' (young upwardly mobile professionals) flaunted their conspicuous consumption and wealth. Internal quarrels concerning policy on Europe cost Margaret Thatcher her premiership. She resigned on 22 November 1990. She was replaced by John Major, who went on to win the general election of 1993. His victory was a crushing defeat for the Labour Party, which seemed past all hope of ever being elected again. The face of British politics had changed irrevocably and it was to take the Labour Party a further four years of painful reorganisation and reform to emerge as a viable political force. During this period, a resilient John Major, dogged by disloyal members of his own party ('bastards') and a catalogue of lurid revelations of varying kinds about ministers and other members of the government, persevered as leader. He is widely acknowledged for having made a great contribution to the new Anglo-Irish Agreement that culminated in the Good Friday Talks of 1998. The Labour Party won the general election of 1997.

The stability of Europe, the problems in the Middle East and the fundamental domestic issues of education, health, housing and unemployment are still very much at the centre of debate. The dawn of a new millennium has continued in the same vein of optimism and trepidation that has been a feature of Carol Ann Duffy's life so far. The attack on the World Trade Center in New York on 11 September 2001 and the second war in the Gulf, with all its attendant political fallout, are still sending ripples of doubt through an erstwhile united New Labour Party. George W. Bush's re-election as president of the USA has done nothing to assuage many people's fears concerning the stability of the world. Others, though, believe that he is a strong, positive influence.

CHECK THE NET

One of the most significant inquiries in terms of domestic politics is the inquiry into the events of Sunday 30 January 1972, when thirteen civilians were shot in Belfast by the British army; for more details see **http://www. bloody-sunday-inquiry.org**

LITERARY BACKGROUND

The work of others influences almost all writers, and Carol Ann Duffy is no exception. We may distinguish between what might be termed a traditional English poetic consciousness and her wide reading in European, particularly modernist, writers.

CONTEXT

André Breton's discussion of the meaning, aims and political position of the **surrealist** movement is well worth reading, as Duffy became very interested in its concerns through her friendship with the poet Adrian Henri. Breton's *Manifestos of Surrealism* is translated by Richard Seaver and Helen R. Lane (1969).

As a very young person she would consciously imitate John Keats, a poet for whom she continued to have a high regard into adulthood. This affinity may be discerned in the sensualism of many of her poems, something for which Keats is well known. In the 1970s she was influenced by the Liverpool Poets, with whom she was closely associated, particularly Adrian Henri (1932–2000), who was also an artist. The emphasis given to performance by the Liverpool Poets has since proved to be a key factor in making poetry more popular and accessible. The flourishing of 'The Mersey Sound' coincided with the publication of *Penguin Modern Poets*, a project that brought poetry to a great many people. Penguin Books revived the project in the 1990s. Duffy appears in Volume 2 along with two other women poets, Eavan Boland (1944–) and Vicki Feaver (1943–).

Other poets who were influential in her development were the French Symbolists, Charles Baudelaire (1821–67), Stéphane Mallarmé (1842–98) and Arthur Rimbaud (1854–91); William Wordsworth (1770–1850); W. B. Yeats (1865–1939); Samuel Beckett (1906–89); T. S. Eliot; and W. H. Auden. Robert Browning was a crucial part of Carol Ann Duffy's reading and his *Dramatis Personae* (1864) clearly provided an important example of the **dramatic monologue** form. Among the poets admired by Duffy are Gerard Manley Hopkins (1844–89), Louis MacNeice (1907–63), Michael Longley (1939–) and Seamus Heaney (1939–).

The American poet Adrienne Rich (1929–) has been influential, particularly with regard to ideas about language, which relate directly to her radical lesbian feminism. Laura (Riding) Jackson (1901–91) has been read with interest by Duffy, as have Stevie Smith (1902–71), Emily Dickinson (1830–86), Charlotte Mew (1869–1928), Sylvia Plath (1932–63), May Swenson (1913–89) and Elizabeth Bishop (1911–79).

While at university, the philosophy of Ludwig Wittgenstein (1889–1951) made a strong impression on Duffy. His ideas about language inevitably attracted a developing poet. Wittgenstein's *Tractatus* and *Philosophical Investigations* are of particular interest. The *Tractatus*, published in 1922 (the same year as James Joyce's

Ulysses and T. S. Eliot's *The Waste Land*), deals with the ability of language to say anything reliable and this is a theme that preoccupies Duffy in several poems.

Although the primary focus here is upon literary influence it is impossible to neglect the impact of the visual arts in Duffy's work. Artists in Europe had at least as strong an impact on modernism as writers. The work of the surrealists and cubists was particularly notable. The link between Duffy's work and paintings is clear in several poems. Examples of these are 'Standing Female Nude', 'Poem in Oils' (*Standing Female Nude*), and the 'Three Paintings' triptych (*Selling Manhattan*). In these poems may be seen the influence of Georges Braque, Max Ernst, Pablo Picasso and René Magritte. Some of Carol Ann Duffy's poems use paintings by these artists as a starting point for a poem or employ **imagery** that owes something to their representational techniques.

MODERNISM

The artistic and literary movement that came to be known as modernism is difficult to define precisely, but we may confidently say that it coincided with a tremendous change in religious, philosophical and artistic outlook following the end of the First World War in 1918. The Georgian school, which included poets such as Rupert Brooke, really had little left to say in the face of the trenches. It would be fatuous, though, to suggest that all the elements of modernism suddenly appeared.

The changes followed the publication of Charles Darwin's *Origin of Species* in 1859, and the decline in religious faith as exemplified in poets such as Charles Algernon Swinburne in England and Charles Baudelaire in France. Baudelaire's *Les Fleurs du Mal* (1857) was a powerful influence, not least on T. S. Eliot. Stéphane Mallarmé in France contributed to an intellectual atmosphere that paved the way for the influential figures of the twentieth century. Matthew Arnold in his poem 'Dover Beach' (1867) famously wrote about the sea of faith ebbing.

The horror of the Great War left many people questioning the possibility of the existence of a benign God. Philosophers such as

 CHECK THE NET

For a commentary on modernism, search **http://www. poetrymagic. co.uk**

the Frenchman Jean-Paul Sartre (1905–80) developed the philosophical position that came to be widely known as existentialism. Its adherents included the poet and novelist Albert Camus (1913–60). Other writers and thinkers subscribed to this position.

Perhaps the most seismic contribution to modernism was made in 1922, the year in which both *Ulysses* by James Joyce and *The Waste Land* by T. S. Eliot were published. James Joyce's novel was considered so scandalous in Ireland that he was forced to have it published in Paris. One of its most celebrated features is its employment of a writing technique that has come to be termed stream of consciousness. It replicates the ebb and flow of thought patterns as they occur, escaping the imposition of conventional linear narrative. Virginia Woolf's *To the Lighthouse* (1927) is another notable example of a novel employing this technique.

CONTEXT

Stream of consciousness is a writing technique that attempts to convey all the contents of a character's mind in relation to the stream of experience as it passes by, often at random.

T. S. Eliot was himself profoundly influenced by the French Symbolist poets. Ezra Pound (1885–1972), whose *Cantos* stands as one of the most admired poetic achievements of the century, was closely associated with T. S. Eliot, who dedicated *The Waste Land* to him with the words '*il miglior fabbro*', the Italian for 'the better maker'. Just as James Joyce's prose allowed for the exploration of consciousness in a free associative way, T. S. Eliot's adoption of **free verse** or ***vers libre*** allowed him to escape traditional poetic forms. His technique of what amounts to cultural collage coupled with the use of **dramatic monologue** was very influential. He had considered calling *The Waste Land* 'He Do the Police in Different Voices', something that clearly stresses his regard for the dramatic in verse, not to mention his regard for Dickens's *Our Mutual Friend*, from which his alternative title is a quotation. His verse plays such as *Murder in the Cathedral* (1935) are further testament to this. Another highly influential poet was W. B. Yeats. Although a modern, he resisted free verse, finding traditional forms more suited to what he had to say.

In the world of theatre, a group of dramatists that included Eugène Ionesco (1912–94), Luigi Pirandello (1867–1936) and Samuel

Beckett (1906–89) wrote plays that came to be referred to as part of the Theatre of the Absurd, a term popularised by the critic Martin Esslin. In musical terms, Igor Stravinsky's *The Rite of Spring* (1913) is counted as a modernist piece.

FEMINISM

The term feminism has been variously misrepresented or misunderstood, not least by some who claim to subscribe to its principles. On a very basic level it might be defined as a way of thinking which requires women to be treated as human beings in their own right and not simply as adjuncts or servants of men.

Three categories of feminism are often discussed: radical feminism, Marxist feminism and liberal feminism. There is sometimes conflict among what emerges as factionalism in feminism at the start of the twenty-first century. Radical feminists would argue that the liberals assume that women have gained more ground than is actually the case and that active measures should be taken if necessary. They are less conciliatory towards men and are wary of the patriarchy they see as a constant threat. Marxist feminism draws attention to the power structures in society and their basic relationship with economics. An increasing number of women in positions of responsibility and who are financially independent have been free to make choices in life, leading the Marxists to argue that their polemic has yielded results. The rather crude distinctions made here do not really reflect the true situation, since there are many women who would align themselves with different facets of its discourse at different times and for differing reasons.

It seems incredible now to think that women were not allowed to vote in Britain until 1928. Christabel Pankhurst (1880–1958), daughter of Emmeline, was largely responsible for securing the enfranchisement of women. She had called a suffrage truce during the First World War and helped to lead the war effort. It is salutary to remember, too, that a campaign of hunger strikes and open-air rallies had been necessary to bring the treatment of women as second-class citizens into the arena of serious debate. What came to be known as the Women's Movement in the 1960s began with such groups as the suffragettes.

 **CHECK THE NET**

Search the online encyclopedia Wikipedia – **http://en.wikipedia.org** – for more information about recent political events both in Britain and elsewhere in the world. There are some very detailed year-by-year timelines that cover cultural and social events, as well as political affairs.

FEMINISM continued

CHECK THE BOOK

Germaine Greer's seminal feminist text, *The Female Eunuch*, first published in 1970, heralded a new age in feminist views of women's experience.

Seminal feminist texts such as Germaine Greer's *The Female Eunuch* (1970) advocated sexual freedom for women. In it she argued that the passivity of women's sexuality is to result in the female equivalent of the role of a castrate, a man who has been emasculated. Her latest contribution, *The Whole Woman* (1999), returns to the issue of women's rights. Greer said in early 1999 that 'it's time to get angry again', indicating that she believes the battle for true equality is not yet won. Clearly, then, feminism is inextricably bound up with politics or, more specifically, sexual politics. Bearing this in mind, we come to the feminist perspective on literary theory.

Any text may be interrogated from a variety of perspectives (see **Critical history** and **Further reading**). The feminist viewpoint starts with the premise that **phallocentric**, patriarchal structures underpin society and should be challenged. It would be unwise to ignore the validity of such criticism but it would be an act of equal folly to suggest that any text can be read only in one way. In the case of Carol Ann Duffy's work it would be oversimplifying the case to suggest that she is primarily a feminist – she is a poet. Perhaps this is the most important achievement of the feminist movement as far as poetry is concerned. A woman may be termed a poet on equal terms with a man. The Irish poet Eavan Boland in her book *Object Lessons: The Life of the Woman and the Poet in Our Time* says: 'Ideology is unambiguous; poetry is not. As a younger poet I had discovered that feminism had wonderful strengths as a critique and almost none as an aesthetic' (p. 236). This is a particularly illuminating comment in connection with Duffy's work. Feminism is primarily an **ideological** position and to categorise a poet such as Duffy in such a narrow fashion would be seriously to delimit our appreciation of her aesthetic. While she certainly is a feminist, she writes not simply (to adapt Wordsworth) as a woman speaking to men but as a poet capable of transcending gender boundaries and one whose 'Plainsong' is polyphonic. Eavan Boland again has something important to say in this context:

It stands to reason that the project of the woman poet, connected as it is by dark bonds to the object she once was, cannot make a continuum with the sexualised erotic of the male poem …

*(Object Lessons: The Life of the Woman
and the Poet in Our Time,* p. 232)

Eavan Boland's basic thesis is that in making women the subject of poems, men in fact reduce them to sexualised objects in art. She goes on to say:

I have come to believe that the woman poet is an emblematic figure in poetry now in the same way that the modernist and romantic poets once were. And for the same reasons. Not because she is awkward and daring and disruptive but because – like the modernist and romantic poets in their time – she internalises the stresses and truths of poetry at a particular moment. Her project therefore is neither marginal nor specialist. It is a project that concerns all of poetry, all that leads into it in the past and everywhere it is going in the future.

*(Object Lessons: The Life of the Woman
and the Poet in Our Time,* p. 232)

This is a challenging statement and certainly equates with the strength and what will undoubtedly remain the distinctive voice of women's poetry in general, and Carol Ann Duffy's in particular.

**CHECK
THE BOOK**
Eavan Boland's
*Object Lessons: The
Life of the Woman
and the Poet in Our
Time* (1996)
discusses what it is
to be a woman, Irish
and a poet. She
manages to do this
without directly
mentioning Seamus
Heaney once,
although Yeats
is co-opted
occasionally.

World events

1979 Margaret Thatcher becomes prime minister

1983 Conservative Party wins second term in office

1984 Miners' strike; IRA bomb explodes in Brighton during Conservative Party Conference

1986 Nuclear accident at Chernobyl power plant in the Ukraine

1988 Lockerbie Pan Am jumbo jet blown up; 281 die

1989 Tiananmen Square killings in China; demolition of Berlin Wall begins; Ayatollah Khomeini pronounces 'fatwa' on Salman Rushdie

Carol Ann Duffy

1982 *Fifth Last Song*; *Take My Husband* (play)
1983 'Whoever She Was' wins first prize in National Poetry Competition
1984 *Cavern of Dreams* (play)

1985 *Standing Female Nude* published and wins a Scottish Arts Council Book Award

1986 *Thrown Voices*; *Little Women, Big Boys* (play); *Loss* (radio play)

1987 *Selling Manhattan*

1988 Somerset Maugham Award

1989 Dylan Thomas Award

Literary events

1984 Death of Sir John Betjeman; Ted Hughes appointed Laureate

1985 *Collected Poems* by Norman MacCaig; *Elegies* by Douglas Dunn wins Whitbread Poetry Award
1986 *The Incident Book* by Fleur Adcock; *Making Cocoa for Kingsley Amis* by Wendy Cope; *Badlands* by Elaine Feinstein; *Stet* by Peter Reading wins Whitbread Poetry Award
1987 *A Watching Brief* by U. A. Fanthorpe; *The Haw Lantern* by Seamus Heaney wins Whitbread Poetry Award
1988 *April Galleons* by John Ashbery; *The Automatic Oracle* (1987) by Peter Porter wins Whitbread Poetry Award
1989 *Zoom!* by Simon Armitage; *A New Path to the Waterfall* by Raymond Carver; *Tributes* by Elizabeth Jennings

World events

1990 Violent demonstrations in London against the poll tax; Mrs Thatcher resigns, and John Major becomes prime minister

1991 Gulf War; outbreak of civil war in Yugoslavia; Robert Maxwell drowns

1992 General election: Conservatives re-elected; outbreak of civil war in Bosnia

1994 Tony Blair elected leader of Labour Party; Nelson Mandela becomes president of South Africa

1997 Labour Party wins general election; death of Diana, Princess of Wales

1998 Good Friday talks

Carol Ann Duffy

1990 *The Other Country* published and wins a Scottish Arts Council Book Award

1992 *William and the Ex-Prime Minister*; *I Wouldn't Thank You for a Valentine* (editor); wins Cholmondeley Award

1993 *Mean Time* published and wins the Forward Poetry Prize and the Whitbread Poetry Award

1994 *Selected Poems*

1995 Lannan Literary Award; teaches at Wake Forest University, North Carolina; awarded an OBE; daughter Ella born

1996 *Grimm Tales* with Tim Supple; *Stopping for Death* (editor); *Anvil New Poems* (editor)

1997 *More Grimm Tales*

1998 *The Pamphlet*

Literary events

1990 *Outside History* by Eavan Boland; *City Music* by Elaine Feinstein; *Omeros* by Derek Walcott; Octavia Paz wins Nobel Prize for Literature

1991 *Time-Zones* by Fleur Adcock; *Explaining Magnetism* by Maura Dooley; *Collected Poems* by Les Murray

1992 *Kid* by Simon Armitage; *Serious Concerns* by Wendy Cope; *The Gaze of the Gorgon* by Tony Harrison; *Times and Seasons* by Elizabeth Jennings; *Phrase Book* by Jo Shapcott; Derek Walcott wins Nobel Prize for Literature

1993 *Friend of Heraclitus* by Patricia Beer; *Angel* by Ruth Padel

1994 November 6: Britain's first National Poetry Day; *The Stinking Rose* by Sujata Bhatt; *In a Time of Violence* by Eavan Boland

1995 *Ghost Train* by Sean O'Brien wins Forward Poetry Prize; Seamus Heaney wins Nobel Prize for Literature

1998 *Birthday Letters* by Ted Hughes

World events

1999 Kosovo crisis

2000 Millennium celebrations; Air France Concorde crashes; 118 Russian submariners drown after *Kursk* sinks

2001 Labour Party wins second term in general election; George W. Bush succeeds Bill Clinton as US president; terrorist attack on World Trade Center
2002 Queen Elizabeth II's golden jubilee; introduction of the euro in twelve European countries; weapons inspectors led by Hans Blix arrive in Iraq
2003 Second Gulf War; Saddam Hussein captured

2004 George W. Bush re-elected US president; earthquake and resulting tsunami devastates parts of southern Asia

Carol Ann Duffy

1999 *The World's Wife*; *Five Finger Piglets* with Brian Patten, Roger McGough, Jackie Kay, Gareth Owen and Peter Bailey; *Meeting Midnight*; *Rumpelstiltskin and Other Grimm Tales*; *Time's Tidings* (editor); made a Fellow of the Royal Society of Literature
2000 *The Oldest Girl in the World*; awarded five-year fellowship by the National Endowment of Science, Technology and the Arts (NESTA)
2001 *Hand in Hand* (editor); awarded a CBE

2002 *Feminine Gospels*

2003 *The Good Child's Guide to Rock 'n' Roll*

2004 *New Selected Poems 1984–2004*; *Overheard on a Saltmarsh* (editor); *Out of Fashion* (editor)

Literary events

1999 Death of Ted Hughes; Andrew Motion appointed Laureate; *Killing Time* by Simon Armitage

2000 Death of Adrian Henri

2001 *Downriver* by Sean O'Brien wins Forward Poetry Prize

2003 *Collected Poems* by Roger McGough; *Landing Light* by Don Paterson wins Whitbread Poetry Award and T. S. Eliot Prize
2004 *Corpus* by Michael Symmons Roberts wins Whitbread Poetry Award

Simone de Beauvoir, *The Second Sex*, trans. H. M. Parshley, Penguin, 1974

Bruno Bettelheim, *The Uses of Enchantment: The Meaning and Importance of Fairy Tales*, Peregrine, 1978
  An engrossing psychoanalytical study of fairy tales

Eavan Boland, *Object Lessons: The Life of the Woman and the Poet in Our Time*, Vintage, 1996
  An excellent and highly readable examination of the place of women poets in society

André Breton, *Manifestos of Surrealism*, trans. Richard Seaver and Helen R. Lane, University of Michigan Press, 1969

Angla Carter, *The Bloody Chamber and Other Stories*, Vintage, 1995

Hélène Cixous, 'The Laugh of the Medusa', *Signs I*, 4 (Summer 1976), pp. 875–93

Jeni Couzyn, ed., *The Bloodaxe Book of Contemporary Women Poets: Eleven British Writers*, Bloodaxe, 1985

Gerard Durozoi, *History of the Surrealism Movement*, trans. Alison Anderson, University of Chicago Press, 2002

Terry Eagleton, *Literary Theory: An Introduction*, Blackwell, 1996

Steve Ellis, *The English Eliot: Design, Language and Landscape in 'Four Quartets'*, Routledge, 1991

Linda France, ed., *Sixty Women Poets*, Bloodaxe, 1993

Germaine Greer, *The Female Eunuch*, Flamingo, 1999 (first published 1970)

Germaine Greer, *The Whole Woman*, 1999

Michael Hulse, David Kennedy and David Morley, eds., *The New Poetry*, Bloodaxe, 1993

Phillis Levin, ed., *The Penguin Book of the Sonnet: 500 Years of a Classic Tradition in English*, Penguin, 2001

Angelica Michelis and Antony Rowland, eds., *The Poetry of Carol Ann Duffy: 'Choosing Tough Words'*, Manchester University Press, 2003
  This is the first collection of critical essays on Duffy's work and offers a wide variety of critical perspectives

Toril Moi, *Sexual/Textual Politics: Feminist Literary Theory*, Methuen, 1985

Sean O'Brien, *The Deregulated Muse: Essays on Contemporary British and Irish Poetry*, Bloodaxe, 1998

Don Paterson, ed., *101 Sonnets: From Shakespeare to Heaney*, Faber, 1999

Deryn Rees-Jones, *Carol Ann Duffy* (Writers and Their Work), Northcote House, 1999
  A fine, concise study of Carol Ann Duffy's achievement

Adrienne Rich, *The Dream of a Common Language: Poems 1974–1977*, Norton, 1978

Adrienne Rich, *Collected Early Poems 1950–1970*, Norton, 1993

Adrienne Rich, *Dark Fields of the Republic: Poems 1991–1995*, Norton, 1995

Ferdinand de Saussure, *Course in General Linguistics*, trans. Roy Harris, Duckworth, 1995

Michael Schmidt, *Lives of the Poets*, Weidenfeld & Nicolson, 1998
  A jargon-free survey of poets through the centuries that helps to place Carol Ann Duffy and her contemporaries in context

Peter Schwenger, *Phallic Critiques: Masculinity and Twentieth-Century Literature*, Routledge, 1984

William Shakespeare, *Sonnets*, ed. Katherine Duncan-Jones, Arden, 1997

Jane E. Thomas, '"The Intolerable Wrestle with Words": The Poetry of Carol Ann Duffy', *Bête Noire*, 6 (Winter 1998), pp. 78–88

Margaret Willy, *Browning's Men and Women*, Macmillan, 1968

Ludwig Wittgenstein, *Tractatus Logico-Philosophicus*, trans. C. K. Ogden, Routledge, 1981

Virginia Woolf, *A Room of One's Own*, Granada Publishing Ltd, 1977
  An important work that has influenced many women writers

alliteration a sequence of repeated consonantal sounds in a stretch of language. The matching consonants are usually at the beginning of words or stressed syllables

allusion a passing reference in a work of literature to something outside itself. A writer may allude to legends, historical facts or personages, to other works of literature, or even to autobiographical details

ambiguity the capacity of words and sentences to have double, multiple or uncertain meanings. A **pun** is the simplest example of ambiguity, where a word is used so as to have two sharply different possible meanings, usually with comic or wry effect

ambivalence ambiguity of feeling; the coexistence of two different attitudes to the same object

anaphora a rhetorical device, common in prose, verse and speech, in which a word or phrase is repeated in several successive clauses

apologist someone who argues a case for a set of beliefs

argot often used to describe the **slang** used by those disapproved of by society

artifice refers either to the skill of the writer in contriving a work of art, or to the work of art itself. The word draws attention to the fact that the world of art and literature is a construct, not the same as the real world

assonance the correspondence, or near correspondence, in two words of the stressed vowel; the line 'on these lips; my body now a softer rhyme' in 'Anne Hathaway' (*The World's Wife*) is an example of this

avant-garde a term used to describe modern artists or writers whose works are (or were) deliberately experimental

cadence a rhythm which coincides with a conclusion or finishing effect. For example, the concluding line of 'Prayer' (*Mean Time*): 'Rockall. Malin. Dogger. Finisterre.'

cliché a word or phrase that has lost its impact because of overuse

closure the way in which the syntax of a piece of verse can coincide with the metrical unit, either in the case of a line (when it is 'end-stopped') or a stanza. For example, the final line of 'Prayer' (*Mean Time*) – 'Rockall. Malin. Dogger. Finisterre' – is end-stopped and end-rhymed. An even stronger sense of closure is achieved since Carol Ann Duffy employs **enjambment** extensively in the three **quatrains** of the **sonnet** and the expectation built up by this is denied by the poem's ending

conceit originally 'conceit' meant simply a thought or an opinion. The distinguishing quality of a conceit is that it should forge an unexpected comparison between two apparently dissimilar things or ideas. Carol Ann Duffy compares an onion and the nature of love in 'Valentine' (*Mean Time*)

connotation the various secondary meanings and overtones of a word: that which it suggests and implies rather than means. The connotations of words make **metaphor** possible

consonance repeated arrangements of consonants, with a change in the vowel that separates them: 'snog' and 'snags' in 'The Captain of the 1964 *Top of the Form* Team' (*Mean Time*) is an example of consonance

couplet a pair of rhymed lines, of any metre. 'Anne Hathaway' (*The World's Wife*) finishes with a rhyming couplet: 'I hold him in the casket of my widow's head / as he held me upon that next best bed.'

dactyl a metrical foot comprising a strongly stressed syllable, followed by two weak ones: tum-ti-ti, as in the word 'strawberry'

demotic in English a style based on the language of ordinary speech, and intended to be readily comprehensible to ordinary people

dialect in most European languages the particular style and manner of speaking of one particular area

diction the choice of words in a work of literature; the kind of vocabulary used

didacticism didactic literature is designed to instruct or to persuade

dramatic monologue a poem in which a single person, not the poet, is speaking

eclectic drawing upon a large number of sources or influences

ellipsis in grammar, the omission of words thought to be essential in the complete form of the sentence. The punctuation mark also known as ellipsis (three dots) can be used to indicate passage of time as well as omission

enjambment the term used to describe a line of poetry which is not end-stopped, that is to say, in which the sentence continues into the next line without any pause being necessary to clarify the grammar, and therefore without any punctuation mark

etymology the study of the history and origins of words, and their changing forms and meanings

euphemism a word or phrase that is less blunt, rude or terrifying than that which it replaces

feminine rhyme rhymed words of two or more syllables, when the last syllable is not stressed: finding / grinding, ladle / cradle

free verse or *vers libre* poetry that is released from the convention of metre and cannot easily be resolved into regular lines of repeated feet that characterise traditional versification

half-rhyme imperfect rhyme – 'live' and 'love' are a half-rhyme in 'Away and See' (*Mean Time*)

hyperbole a figure of speech in which exaggeration is used for rhetorical effect

iambic a term to describe a rhythm in poetry based upon feet of two syllables in which a weak stress is followed by a strong stress

ideology generally speaking, the collection of ideas, values, beliefs and preconceptions which go to make up the discourse of a group of people; the framework through which they view everything; what we take to be 'reality' is controlled by the ideologies of the age in which we live

image, imagery in its narrowest sense an image is a word picture. More commonly, however, imagery refers to the figurative language in a piece of literature

internal rhyme a pair of words rhyming within a line of verse; 'slice of ice' in 'Stealing' (*Selling Manhattan*) is an internal rhyme

irony saying or writing one thing but implying another

Jungian based on the ideas of the psychologist Carl Gustav Jung (1875–1961), who argued that men have a female side he called the anima and women have a male side of their personalities called the animus

kenning (Old Norse 'know, recognise') a stock **metaphoric** phrase in the oral poetry of Scandinavia and in Anglo-Saxon verse. An Old English example is hran-rad ('whale-road'). The example from 'Selling Manhattan' (*Selling Manhattan*) is 'firewater'

lyric a poem that is neither narrative nor dramatic. A more particularised definition describes a lyric as a poem, usually short, expressing in a personal manner the feelings and thoughts of an individual speaker (not necessarily those of the poet). The typical lyric subject matter is love. 'Words, Wide Night' (*The Other Country*) is a lyric

masculine rhyme a poetic line ending on an accented or stressed syllable

metaphor a figure of speech in which one thing is described as being another thing

metaphysical poets metaphysics is the philosophy of being and knowing, but this term was originally applied to a group of seventeenth-century poets in a derogatory manner. The poets included Donne, Herbert, Marvell, Vaughan, Crashaw and Carew. Their poems are characterised by witty displays of ingenious **conceits**, clever paradoxes and **puns**, and language with a wide range of **metaphorical** association

myth a story, usually concerning superhumans or gods, which is related to or attempts to explain religious beliefs: myths originate far back in the culture of oral societies. Writers of almost all ages have valued myths and used them for literary purposes long after the stories have ceased to have any religious content. Carol Ann Duffy uses a wide range of classical myths in *The World's Wife*

onomatopoeic words which sound like the noise they describe. Carol Ann Duffy uses 'fizzing' to describe the optimism felt by the **persona** in 'The Captain of the 1964 *Top of the Form* Team' (*Mean Time*)

oxymoron a figure of speech in which contradictory terms are brought together in what is at first sight an impossible combination. Examples in Carol Ann Duffy's poetry are 'Love's / hate' in 'Havisham' (*Mean Time*) and 'living dead' in 'Never Go Back' (*Mean Time*)

pathetic fallacy assuming that there is an equation between human mood and the external world

pathos a word to describe moments in works or art which evoke strong feelings of pity and sorrow

persona derived from the Latin 'mask' and used by writers to present the point of view of a person who is clearly not the writer

personification a variety of figurative language in which things or ideas are treated as if they were human beings, with human attributes and feeling. The 'laugh of a bell' in 'In Mrs Tilscher's Class' (*The Other Country*) is an example of personification

phallocentric a feminist term to describe the way societies are organised according to masculine values

pun usually defined as 'a play on words', it usually draws out two widely different meanings from a single word. The purpose of the pun is usually comic but it can be used in more serious ways

quatrain a stanza of four lines

register used by critics to denote 'a kind of language being used', especially the kind of language appropriate to a particular situation

rhyme chiming or matching sounds at the ends of lines of verse which create an audible sense of pattern

satire literature which exhibits or examines vice and folly and makes them appear ridiculous or contemptible

sign noise or mark on paper

signified the meaning to which the **sign** refers

simile a figure of speech in which one thing is said to be like another and the comparison is made with the use of 'like' or 'as'

slang colloquial language of a racy, informal kind; sometimes offensive or abusive language. Carol Ann Duffy uses cockney rhyming slang in 'The Kray Sisters' (*The World's Wife*) where 'Vera Lynn', for example, stands for 'gin'

sonnet a **lyric** poem of fourteen lines of **iambic** pentameter rhymed and organised according to several intricate schemes. The Italian poet Petrarch (1304–74) established the sonnet as a major poetic form in his *Canzoniere* (c.1335). Petrarchan or Italian sonnets are divided into octave and sestet, rhymes *abbaabba cde cde* (or *cdcdcd*); Shakespearean sonnets are divided into three **quatrains** and a **couplet**, rhymed *abab cdcd efef gg*. Carol Ann Duffy does not always follow traditional rhyme schemes in her sonnets and she does not always put them to lyrical use (see **Poetic form: The sonnet**)

stereotype a standard, fixed idea or mental impression

surrealism an artistic and literary movement starting in France in the 1920s which drew upon the concepts of Freudian psychology. The influence of surrealism is evident in a number of Carol Ann Duffy's poems

symbol something that represents something else, by analogy or **allusion**. In 'Valentine' (*Mean Time*) a wedding ring becomes symbolic of death for Carol Ann Duffy, something she associated with marriage at the time

tone in conveying tone, words can suggest the sense of a particular manner or mood in which a passage should be read

vers libre see **free verse**

volta the change in mood and argument which occurs between the octave and sestet of a **sonnet**

AUTHOR OF THESE NOTES

Michael J. Woods is Assistant Headteacher at The Chase Technology College in Malvern, Worcestershire. He edits and publishes *Tandem* poetry magazine and has completed academic research on the poetry of Gerard Manley Hopkins.

General editor

Martin Gray, former Head of the Department of English Studies at the University of Stirling, and of Literary Studies at the University of Luton

NOTES

Maya Angelou
I Know Why the Caged Bird Sings

Jane Austen
Pride and Prejudice

Alan Ayckbourn
Absent Friends

Elizabeth Barrett Browning
Selected Poems

Robert Bolt
A Man for All Seasons

Harold Brighouse
Hobson's Choice

Charlotte Brontë
Jane Eyre

Emily Brontë
Wuthering Heights

Shelagh Delaney
A Taste of Honey

Charles Dickens
David Copperfield
Great Expectations
Hard Times
Oliver Twist

Roddy Doyle
Paddy Clarke Ha Ha Ha

George Eliot
Silas Marner
The Mill on the Floss

Anne Frank
The Diary of a Young Girl

William Golding
Lord of the Flies

Oliver Goldsmith
She Stoops to Conquer

Willis Hall
The Long and the Short and the Tall

Thomas Hardy
Far from the Madding Crowd
The Mayor of Casterbridge
Tess of the d'Urbervilles
The Withered Arm and other Wessex Tales

L.P. Hartley
The Go-Between

Seamus Heaney
Selected Poems

Susan Hill
I'm the King of the Castle

Barry Hines
A Kestrel for a Knave

Louise Lawrence
Children of the Dust

Harper Lee
To Kill a Mockingbird

Laurie Lee
Cider with Rosie

Arthur Miller
The Crucible
A View from the Bridge

Robert O'Brien
Z for Zachariah

Frank O'Connor
My Oedipus Complex and Other Stories

George Orwell
Animal Farm

J.B. Priestley
An Inspector Calls
When We Are Married

Willy Russell
Educating Rita
Our Day Out

J.D. Salinger
The Catcher in the Rye

William Shakespeare
Henry IV Part I
Henry V
Julius Caesar
Macbeth
The Merchant of Venice
A Midsummer Night's Dream
Much Ado About Nothing

Romeo and Juliet
The Tempest
Twelfth Night

George Bernard Shaw
Pygmalion

Mary Shelley
Frankenstein

R.C. Sherriff
Journey's End

Rukshana Smith
Salt on the snow

John Steinbeck
Of Mice and Men

Robert Louis Stevenson
Dr Jekyll and Mr Hyde

Jonathan Swift
Gulliver's Travels

Robert Swindells
Daz 4 Zoe

Mildred D. Taylor
Roll of Thunder, Hear My Cry

Mark Twain
Huckleberry Finn

James Watson
Talking in Whispers

Edith Wharton
Ethan Frome

William Wordsworth
Selected Poems

A Choice of Poets

Mystery Stories of the Nineteenth Century including The Signalman

Nineteenth Century Short Stories

Poetry of the First World War

Six Women Poets

For the AQA Anthology:

Duffy and Armitage & Pre-1914 Poetry

Heaney and Clarke & Pre-1914 Poetry

Poems from Different Cultures

Margaret Atwood
Cat's Eye
The Handmaid's Tale

Jane Austen
Emma
Mansfield Park
Persuasion
Pride and Prejudice
Sense and Sensibility

Alan Bennett
Talking Heads

William Blake
Songs of Innocence and of Experience

Charlotte Brontë
Jane Eyre
Villette

Emily Brontë
Wuthering Heights

Angela Carter
Nights at the Circus

Geoffrey Chaucer
The Franklin's Prologue and Tale
The Merchant's Prologue and Tale
The Miller's Prologue and Tale
The Prologue to the Canterbury Tales
The Wife of Bath's Prologue and Tale

Samuel Coleridge
Selected Poems

Joseph Conrad
Heart of Darkness

Daniel Defoe
Moll Flanders

Charles Dickens
Bleak House
Great Expectations
Hard Times

Emily Dickinson
Selected Poems

John Donne
Selected Poems

Carol Ann Duffy
Selected Poems

George Eliot
Middlemarch
The Mill on the Floss

T.S. Eliot
Selected Poems
The Waste Land

F. Scott Fitzgerald
The Great Gatsby

E.M. Forster
A Passage to India

Brian Friel
Translations

Thomas Hardy
Jude the Obscure
The Mayor of Casterbridge
The Return of the Native
Selected Poems
Tess of the d'Urbervilles

Seamus Heaney
Selected Poems from 'Opened Ground'

Nathaniel Hawthorne
The Scarlet Letter

Homer
The Iliad
The Odyssey

Aldous Huxley
Brave New World

Kazuo Ishiguro
The Remains of the Day

Ben Jonson
The Alchemist

James Joyce
Dubliners

John Keats
Selected Poems

Philip Larkin
The Whitsun Weddings and Selected Poems

Christopher Marlowe
Doctor Faustus
Edward II

Arthur Miller
Death of a Salesman

John Milton
Paradise Lost Books I & II

Toni Morrison
Beloved

George Orwell
Nineteen Eighty-Four

Sylvia Plath
Selected Poems

Alexander Pope
Rape of the Lock & Selected Poems

William Shakespeare
Antony and Cleopatra
As You Like It
Hamlet
Henry IV Part I
King Lear
Macbeth
Measure for Measure
The Merchant of Venice
A Midsummer Night's Dream
Much Ado About Nothing
Othello
Richard II
Richard III
Romeo and Juliet
The Taming of the Shrew
The Tempest
Twelfth Night
The Winter's Tale

George Bernard Shaw
Saint Joan

Mary Shelley
Frankenstein

Jonathan Swift
Gulliver's Travels and A Modest Proposal

Alfred Tennyson
Selected Poems

Virgil
The Aeneid

Alice Walker
The Color Purple

Oscar Wilde
The Importance of Being Earnest

Tennessee Williams
A Streetcar Named Desire
The Glass Menagerie

Jeanette Winterson
Oranges Are Not the Only Fruit

John Webster
The Duchess of Malfi

Virginia Woolf
To the Lighthouse

William Wordsworth
The Prelude and Selected Poems

W.B. Yeats
Selected Poems

Metaphysical Poets